The Real Ronald Reagan—

A TRUE HUMANITARIAN

THE REAL

Ronald Reagan

A TRUE HUMANITARIAN

Mary Joan Roll-Sieffert

Epic
Press

Belleville, Ontario, Canada

The Real Ronald Reagan—A True Humanitarian
Copyright © 2003, Mary Joan Roll-Sieffert

National Library of Canada Cataloguing in Publication

Roll-Sieffert, Mary Joan, 1933-
    The real Ronald Reagan : a true humanitarian / Mary Joan Roll-
Sieffert.

Includes bibliographical references.
ISBN 1-55306-549-2. — ISBN 1-55306-551-4 (LSI ed.) — ISBN
1-55306-573-5 (hardcover ed.)

    1. Reagan, Ronald. 2. Presidents—United States—Biography. 3.
Motion picture actors and actresses—United States—Biography. 4.
Roll-Sieffert, Mary Joan, 1933- 5. Fans (Persons)—United States.
I. Title.

E877.R654 2003   973.927'092   C2003-900251-9

**For more information or
to order additional copies, please contact:**

Mary Joan Roll-Sieffert
939 Perry Hwy.
Pittsburg, PA 15229-1146

Epic Press is an imprint of *Essence Publishing,* a Christian Book Pub-
lisher dedicated to furthering the work of Christ through the written word.
For more information, contact:
    44 Moira Street West, Belleville, Ontario, Canada K8P 1S3
        Phone: 1-800-238-6376 • Fax: (613) 962-3055
E-mail: info@essencegroup.com • Internet: www.essencegroup.com

Table of Contents

Preface

AS AN ACTOR, Ronald Reagan loved to play a hero, and did play a hero in all but one of his 50 films. As the 40th president of the most powerful nation on Earth, he showed America and the world what a real hero is. Ronald Reagan saw America as a very special place, like a shining beacon instituted by God, a place where mankind can freely engage in the divinely endowed ideals of life, liberty, and the pursuit of happiness.

I truly believe he was this country's hero and with God's saving grace protected his fellow man from an Armageddon-like event that defies the imagination with courage, vision and faith in the American people, and the American dream consummating with the now-legendary statement, "Mr. Gorbachev, tear down this wall!"

It is my wish that all who read the following pages will see in the life of Ronald Reagan what I have seen through the years—a dedicated family man, a talented entertainer, a coura-geous leader, and a true humanitarian.

I would like to thank the following people for their gen-erous support and assistance: Megan Hamm, Jeff Kammersell, Eileen and Harry Hendrickson, Andy Van Gorder, and Joseph Nardi—who proved himself, through his help, a true friend. Also, Jodi Hynes, Lou Hancherick, Stacy J., and my ever-sup-portive brother, Jack Roll.

Introduction

THIS BOOK IS not an exhaustive biographical work on the life of Ronald Reagan. It is, however, a unique look at his life from the perspective of a loyal devotee. Joan Roll-Sieffert, the author, was the president of the Pittsburgh chapter of the Ronald Reagan Fan Club. In that role she stayed in touch with him, from the days he was an aspiring young actor throughout his presidency and beyond—all together, an involvement that spans more than five decades. Joan shares with us in this book her memories of this remarkable man she idolized.

You will find in the pages that follow a treasure trove of photos and fan club memorabilia sure to be coveted by Reagan movie buffs. You will catch an insider's glimpse of the mind and manner of this American hero in his correspondence with Joan. Joan also unabashedly shares her personal viewpoints regarding the historical, humanitarian and spiritual significance of Ronald Reagan's life and presidency. This all adds up to an engaging read with a unique historical bent.

Think of this book as a loving testament to an icon.

Lou Hancherick,
Editor, Harmony Magazine

ONE

Ronald's Early Beginning

HE WAS BORN Ronald Wilson Reagan on February 6, 1911, nicknamed "Dutch" by his father, John Edward Reagan, who was a shoe salesman and managed his own shoe store. His father did have the problem of being an alcoholic.

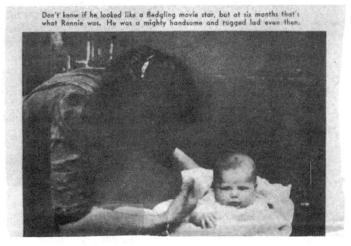

"Don't know if he looked like a fledgling movie star, but at six months that's what Ronnie was. He was a mighty handsome and rugged lad even then"

Ronald at two-years-old

"Moms Nelle"

His mother was Nelle Wilson Reagan, a small woman with auburn hair and blue eyes, who they affectionately called "Moms Nelle." She was very kind and loving to all she associated with and often helped Ronald with his fan mail when he was completely occupied with his work.

1. RONALD REAGAN, here six months old, had made his initial appearance in Tampico, Illinois, on February 6, 1912.

2. REAGAN BROTHERS. Neil, left, and Ronnie, now eight months old. Two years older, Neil went by the name Moon, was our boy's idol.

3. REAGAN FAMILY: father, John Edward; mother, Nell; Moon (left) and Ronnie. Father, called Jack by the kids, eventually became partner in a shoe store in Dixon, Ill., where the boys did their growing up.

4. SCHOOL for Ronnie (center), eight years old and in third grade. 5. (Right) 13-year-old football enthusiast who got low marks in school.

6. FOOTBALL player who still got low marks but played guard (Moon at end) on high school team. Ronnie was five feet, ten inches—160 pounds—light but speedy.

7. EUREKA COLLEGE, guard on football team for three years, playing in every game. Dramatics came next. Journey's End lead, etc.

8. SPORTS ANNOUNCER worked up to Coast-to-Coast NBC broadcasting major league baseball meets, championships.

9. LIFEGUARD and very popular with drowning girls (hundreds, oddly enough) at Lowell Beach. He enjoyed this same job all through high school and college.

Pictures of Ronald from baby to lifeguard and with family [1]

---

[1] Hubler, Richard G., and Ronald Reagan, *Where's the Rest of Me: The Ronald Reagan Story.* (Hollywood: Duell, Sloan and Pearce, Publisher Affiliate of Meredith Press, 1965). A very charitable lady who arranged meetings with various clubs and visited the prisoners in the local jails weekly while living in Illinois. Once she moved to California, she discovered a tuberculosis sanitarium and that became her pet charity where she volunteered regularly.

Ronald, Bessie and Neil

I truly believe her Christian ways were passed on to Ronald as he is a genuine humanitarian with acts of service he did for the benefit of his fellow man. Moms Nelle belonged to a Bible-oriented Christian church. She and Ronald shared the same Christian beliefs.[2] His older brother was named Neil Reagan, nicknamed "Moon" by his father. Neil's wife was named Bessie. They (the original family) moved from Tampico, Illinois, when Ronald was nine years old, to Dixon, Illinois, which is called the Petunia City. It remained his home until he was 21 years old.[3]

After he graduated from high school, he went to Eureka College in Eureka, Illinois. Playing football helped him pay his tuition for his college years.[4] While he was still in high school, he was introduced to drama and acting. While attending Eureka College and playing football, he also became a lifeguard.[5] After working seven summers at Lowell Park in Dixon,

---

[2] Hubler. Elementary school where both Moms Nelle and John Edward Reagan graduated. It was Moms Nelle's opinion that no diploma was needed for kindness.

[3] Hubler. While Ronald attended high school living in Dixon, Illinois, he developed into a gifted athlete. He played basketball, went out for track runner and engaged in swimming.

[4] Hubler.

[5] Hubler.

Illinois, he managed to save 77 people from drowning. He also joined the drama society in college. He graduated from Eureka College in 1932 with a degree in Economics and Sociology. After he graduated from college, he became a sports announcer for the University of Iowa, where he truly enjoyed describing bit by bit every football game played by Iowa University on station WOC. From there he moved on to station WHO in Des Moines, key station for NBC in the Midwest as their sports announcer.

While being a sports announcer for Des Moines WHO, he was offered a screen test from Hollywood. He was then notified he was awarded a contract with Warner Brothers. His next move was to Hollywood, where he later moved his whole family. Moms Nelle wrote me in a letter that he moved all of them to Los Angeles and bought them a beautiful home.

The first movie he made was *Love Is In The Air* in 1937. All of his movies and co-stars will be explained to you in Chapter 4.

In 1938, Ronald was placed on the board of the Screen Actors Guild ("SAG"), where he started his experience in political negotiating. He found himself not only an actor but a true rabid union man as president of the SAG.

According to his mother, Moms Nelle, and I personally agree with her, Ronald's reason for accepting leadership and negotiating in the SAG was that he was terribly grateful for all he had and wanted those good things for others, too.

Ronald met Jane Wyman in 1939. They became engaged in a cross-country tour given by Louella Parsons. That cross-country tour was shown in downtown Pittsburgh in what used to be the Stanley Theater, which is now the Benedum Theater in downtown Pittsburgh.

SO LONG, BUTTON N... Jane and one-
year-old Maureen say ...nie off from their
...rly Hills home. He was Army Captain.

Ron and Jane

Ron and Jane

RONNIE REAGAN, after finally hitting stardom, chucked it all for a lieutenant's commission in the U. S. Cavalry. A crack rider and marksman, he's Reserve-trained like thousands of fellow Americans left behind a week before his lovely wife Jane Wymon

Ron and Jane

They were married in 1940 and had two children, Maureen and Michael. Maureen was born in 1941. Maureen remains a devoted, loving daughter to him as he was her devoted father; Maureen is the one that acknowledges that.

After Jane Wyman experienced a miscarriage, they both adopted Michael in 1945.

He also sent personal pictures of Maureen and Michael as young children and babies.

When a boy and his dad go out walking the whole world is theirs—any adventure at all
can happen, witness the happy expressions on the faces of Ronald and Michael Reagan.

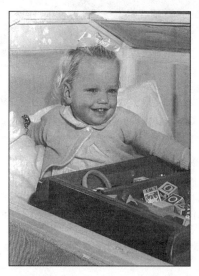

Maureen at seven months old

On Ronald Reagan's return from England where he was doing *The Hasty Heart*, he found daughter Maureen a very grown up young lady of eight, studying ballet with the Ballet Russe de Monte Carlo.

Maureen and Michael

Maureen and Michael

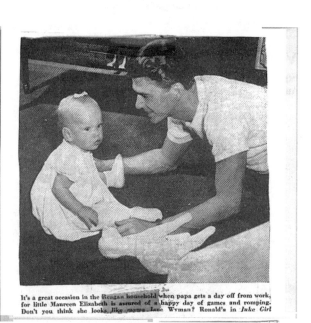

It's a great occasion in the Reagan household when papa gets a day off from work, for little Maureen Elizabeth is assured of a happy day of games and romping. Don't you think she looks like mama Jane Wyman? Ronald's in *Juke Girl*

Maureen playing with her dad

Michael and his dad

Ronnie encourages Mike in everything he does, builds up his self-
confidence. Mike jumps over his grandmother's hedge as Ronnie cheers.

Ronald and Michael

Since seeing him in uniform, Ronald Reagan's daughter, above, who looks a lot like her mother, Jane Wyman, runs after every man in uniform, hoping it's her Daddy. Reagan, a reserve officer in the U. S. Cavalry for five years, was called into active service after completing "Desperate Journey."

Ronald bought his first ranch during this time. He bought his first horse, named Tar Baby, at the same time. You can see pictures of Ronald and Tar Baby. Then, later, he had a horse named Sheila, which he sent an autographed picture of them to me.

Ron with Tar Baby

The ending of this marriage between Ronald and Jane Wyman was very painful for Ronald Reagan. It was painful for his two children as is any divorce between parents to most children. It all ended in 1948.

Ron with his mother, Moms Nelle

Ronald did not enjoy being a bachelor in Hollywood. If you went out on a simple dinner date with someone, the publicity people made it a romance. When anyone asked him about the divorce, he stated the main loss he felt was someone to give his love to. He always cautioned his fans not to believe everything they read about famous celebrities because most of it was not true.

Ronald was called into the U.S. Army[6] in 1942, where he performed duties as a liaison officer (Second Lieutenant) loading convoys. Because of his severe eye problems, nearsightedness, he was exempt from any military action services. His home base in the army was Fort Mason. He was later transferred to the air force, where his first duties involved interviewing applicants for commissions. Then he made training films for the military. He was then promoted to Captain during his air force duties.[7]

Captain Ron

6 Hubler.
7 Hubler.

His next promotion, to Major, was refused by him. He held very high esteem for the warring men in combat and felt it was not proper for him to become a major with all his state-side duties at home. He felt only those in the war zone were worthy of such a promotion. Now, only a true humanitarian would refuse an offer to be made a Major because of his high respect for the warring military men.

A NEW BEGINNING FOR RONALD

Wherever there's a gala party Ronald Reagan gets an invite, and sweet Nancy Davis is ever by his side.

Ron and Nancy

Ron and Nancy

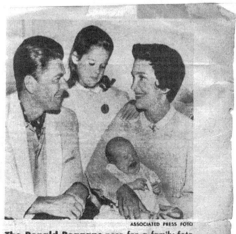

ASSOCIATED PRESS FOTO

The Ronald Reagans pose for a family foto with daughter Patty, 6, and infant son, Ronald.

Ronald and wife Nancy in garden of their new home. With daughter Patty, 2, they're a happy trio. Pop (left) "just happens" to have pictures, too.

It was through the fact that Ronald was president of the SAG that he met his present devoted wife, Nancy Davis.

His first date with Nancy[8] was supposed to be a short one to discuss the problems Nancy was having with MGM. They had to be impressed with each other, because it ended with both of them returning home at 3:30 a.m. Nancy's father was a surgeon and her mother, Edith Luekett, was an actress.[9]

Ronald felt and stated that God was looking out for him by finding Nancy. They stayed together permanently. Throughout Ronald's movie and political years, Nancy remained a dedicated, loving wife to him.

---

[8] Hubler. During their dating days, they both spent time with William Holden and his wife, Ardis, as their close attendants. Ronald and Nancy had their wedding reception at the Holdens' home.

[9] Hubler.

Nancy gave birth to their first baby, Patti, in 1952, by cesarean section. It was after the birth of Patti that they bought their second ranch, much bigger than the first one Ronald owned.

In 1956, they built a beautiful home overlooking the ocean. After time, Nancy became pregnant with their second child, Ronald Prescott. When he, too, was born by cesarean section, Ronald became extremely worried about Nancy having their babies. Ronald Prescott is nicknamed "Skipper." At the time of this birth, Ronald wanted the nurse to tell him first, "Nancy is all right now and in good health," before she told him, "You have a son weighing 8.5 pounds." I'm sure Ronald was gladdened by his son's birth, but his main concern was the health of Nancy during and after the birth. I am sure his son still answers to his nickname, "Skipper," even today.

Nancy, Ronald and Skipper

FURTHER DEVELOPMENT

After appearing in a state play, he was offered the job for "General Electric Theater" on television. He not only introduced all the shows on television, he appeared in some of them. This job led him to personal appearance tours at GE plants throughout his country. The tours were titled "Employers and Community Relations Program." He visited and spoke to 250,000 employees. The speeches that he gave while on tour to the GE plants sometimes ran 14 a day.

Even deep in the heart of London, autograph hounds were hot on the stars' trail. Waitresses, above, spotted Ronald through the window, dashed out still carrying their towels.

On tour for G.E. Theatre

From 1938 starting negotiating for the SAG and later became president. When he became president of the SAG, the employment figures bounced high in Hollywood. Ronald went into action to see to it that the industry accepted its share of responsibility. In a town where politics are dynamic, Ronald's unswerving courage is to be applauded. Another example of his humanitarianism are his efforts to better all actors and actresses in their profession.

PRESIDENT of the Screen Actors' Guild and a star of the first magnitude (*Hasty Heart, Storm Warning,* and *Louisa*) Reagan was toasted—and roasted—by such show-business folk as Al Jolson, Cecil B. DeMille, and George Burns. As vere invited, customary roasting was soft-pedaled.

Ronald as President of the Screen Actors Guild (SAG).

While on tour to all the GE plants in America, it ended up giving him the experience of appearing and lecturing to thousands of different-background people. Even though Ronald Reagan was always portrayed as a hero in all his movies and films, he was destined to be a hero in politics for his fellow man. And no other President of the United States of America had all the experience Ronald had with negotiating and recognizing Communists overtaking while being president of the SAG. He held high esteem for the American people and wanted to downsize government control of all his people, which was his message to thousands while on the GE tours.

It all developed him into a gifted political humanitarian for everyone. While on tour for GE Theater, he was one of the few government leaders that answered truthfully all questions asked after every speech he made to them. Ronald was impressed to all his lectured people as they were with him. I'm sure they remembered the experience with him when he finally ran and became President of the USA.

When he was president of the SAG, he had tremendous experience with Communism infiltrating the motion picture industry. Ronald and his associates did all they could to outrank and preserve the rights of all actors and performers to receive the full benefits they deserved. Ronald gained further experience in dealing with their (Communist's) bargaining tactics and their removal of some peoples' rights. It all gave to Ronald good groundwork in dealing with Communist negotiations, which he used very successfully as president.

What he tried to get through to the public about Communism was that if one group of people in America could be denied fair treatment, then the freedom and rights of all were in danger.

All of his lecturing tours continued until GE Theater was dropped from television in 1962. It gave him a full eight years where he tried enlightening people to the facts about decreasing government control.

Ronald Reagan's handwriting shows him to be a "sincere type," says graphologist Helen King. And that's just the kind of role he has in Warners' gay, "John Loves Mary."

DO YOU WRITE LIKE

Signature of Ronald Reagan

According to Helen King, a handwriting graphologist, his signature (the way he writes his name) is another confirmation that Ronald is a very hard worker with the ability to concentrate and apply his mind to all that is going on. He was always inclined to be optimistic, to look on the brighter side of life with a very logical mind. Ronald never liked wasting time, work, or action. He is also very sensitive, feeling things deeply and sincerely. A very sincere type with the ability to be a good, reliable friend.

All of these characteristics were absolutely confirmed to me being his movie fan and a very appreciative president supporter.

In the book that Ronald's daughter, Patti Davis, wrote about him, called *Angels Don't Die*, she illustrates his Christian faith and found it working for her in her life. It was his gift of faith passed on to her. Patti confirmed that he believed and told her, "Ask and you shall receive, God will answer all your prayers according to God's will for you."

He had the power and the talent to express himself with ease and sincerity. He has been called "The Great Communicator."

Ronald knew when he was being interviewed by someone who was merely looking for defects in his character and seemed to do his best to keep the interview on the subject at hand. When something was written about him that was of a critical nature, I, his fan, often wrote to him inquiring about the nature of the criticism. He would usually follow up with a letter to me telling me the truth about the interview.

So, any interviewer who came up with the opinion that he was not an intelligent, sincere, hard-working man was only trying to confirm their beliefs by giving misquotes that he gave to them to confirm the interviewer's beliefs. They truly did not know the kind, responsible, dedicated character that he truly is. It has truly been sincerely proven to me throughout his early life, being a movie star and being governor of California and, finally, ending up as President of the USA.

TWO

How It All Came Into Being

MY ENTIRE EXPERIENCE with being associated with Ronald Reagan began when I was 14 years old and still in the first half of my high school years. At that time, I was a dedicated movie-goer, living eight blocks from Perry Theater in Pittsburgh. I often walked down to the theater myself; many other times I walked down with my school friends.

There came the right day when I walked into the Perry Theater, sat down and watched a very impressive movie called *Night Unto Night*. It happened to be the film that started my being a fan of Ronald Reagan. He starred in the film with Viveca Linfors. He played a scientist who discovered he had an incurable ailment, epilepsy.

Even now, I remember the *Night Unto Night* Bible quote: "The heavens declare the glory of God; And the firmament showeth his handiwork. Day unto day uttereth speech, And night unto night showeth knowledge" (Psalm 19:1–2, ASV).

The year that *Night Unto Night* was shown was 1947. I started looking for articles about Ronald Reagan in movie magazines. I gained enough interest to join his fan club in

November 1948. You can share with me his personal message he wrote on the back of my membership card. It was his personal message to welcome me into the fan club.

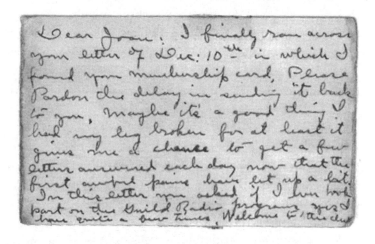

First fan club membership card

I became Pittsburgh Chapter President of his fan club in 1949. At that time, Russie Rae Sell, Rita Ermell, Mary Ann Rupp and Rose Marie Obermier joined with me in paying tribute to Ronald. Later, four others joined us. It was Rita and I who even held charity dances in the name of Ronald Reagan. When you get to the Letters chapter, you will read how he liked the idea and encouraged us to continue holding charity dances in his name.

The official president was Zelda Multz from Brooklyn, New York. The secretary was Lorraine Ruthkowski from Albany, New York. Starting November 1948, I shared a close relationship with Zelda Multz. We became good friends, not only by our letters to each other, but I did manage to travel to New York twice, where I spent some memorable times with her. Lorraine Wagner and Zelda went to Ronald's "Home Coming Indian Summer" celebration along with Moms Nelle.

Ronald with Zelda and Lorraine

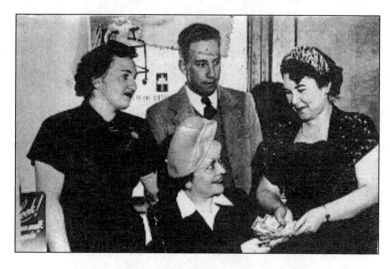

Lorraine Wagner, Moms Nelle, and Zelda Multz

At the same time that I was president of Pittsburgh, there was another president, Lorraine Makler, living in Philadelphia. She later married Elwood Wagner and is now Lorraine Wagner.

Even though I regret never meeting her personally, we became good friends through our correspondence with each other.

Lorraine and her husband, Elwood Wagner, became very important activists in Ronald Reagan's political campaign.

It was through Lorraine that I contacted the Republican party here in Pittsburgh and did volunteer work for them on Ronald's behalf.

I think fondly about Zelda and Lorraine and really want to thank Lorraine again for all the political information she sent to me. You will read Ron's opinions and hopes on the pressing issues at the time of his being

governor of California as well as during his being President of the USA. In August 1999, Lorraine represented Ronald on NBC's television show "The Today Show" as well as being interviewed by *The New Yorker* magazine.

My experience with writing letters became very well-noted. I even had a pen pal from India who was also a fan club member. All of the letters I wrote included two or three letters a month to Ronald. He did answer a lot of my letters with sincere, personal interest, which you can share with me in the Personal Letters chapter.

Ron buying gifts for his friends

Photo postcard from Ronald

Back of postcard

It was quite understandable that between his movie making, being president of the SAG union, while starring and traveling as host of GE Theater, that he had little time to answer every letter written to him. But as you will read later, he did manage to not only personally write letters and post cards, but also to send autographed pictures to me. He sent all his fan club presidents Christmas gifts. To any fan who sent him a gift, I know he returned one, due to his generous nature. Every Christmas, this very appreciative man sent me Christmas presents. I still have a key-and-heart gold necklace plus a beautiful two-strand pearl necklace. Also sent to me were huge candy platters from Los Angeles.

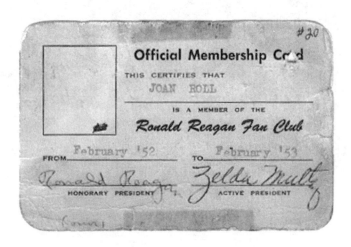

1953 membership card

Ronald tried hard to keep up with his fan mail, even though he was constantly working and traveling. When I received this 1953 membership card, he didn't realize I was a dedicated member for five years. And, as you can read his personal message to me, he was in the hospital after he shattered his leg. He shattered his leg by participating in a charity baseball game played with other actors. Just another example of his humanitarian efforts.

Hospitalized and recovering

He was incapacitated for many months following his accident. A kind-hearted man, he did manage to take the time to show appreciation to his fans.

When Ronald was extremely busy, the only other one that

helped him the most (besides his Moms Nelle) was his sister-in-law, Bessie. Neil's wife, Bessie, was a very thoughtful lady that respected Ronald's fans as much as he did. She always signed her name when she wrote one to me, not pretending it came from Ronald.

All of Ronald's fan club members believed that Ronald's fan club was like one big happy family. It was what democracy was truly meant to be.

My being a fan club member for so long, I became very familiar with Ronald's feelings and opinions, like his favorite song was "Auld Lang Syne."

When asked if he thought a girl had to be thin to be attractive, he stated, "Not at all." When asked what movies and roles he played were his favorites, he replied, "Drake McHugh in *Kings Row*" and then added, "George Gipp in *Knute Rochne* and *Voice of the Turtle*." *Voice of the Turtle* is one of my favorite and admired films.

Ron putting up his guard rail fence

Autographed picture with Sheila

Ronald's favorite pastime was his ranch and being with his horses. He put in his own guardrails and maintained the upkeep of his ranch. He did sometimes have an assistant to help him, but I know he still did most of the work required to keep it in good operating condition.

THEATER GUILD STARS HERE—

Ron and Betty Hutton

I personally met Ronald on May 21, 1950. He starred in a stage play with Betty Hutton, called *The Theater Guild on the Air* at KDKA Syria Mosque. Ron and Betty both stayed at the Schenley Hotel in Oakland. It is now owned by the University of Pittsburgh for their students and additional classrooms.

When Ronald entered the hotel, I was waiting at the door for him because his mother, Moms Nelle, wrote me a letter regarding the time and place he would be in Pittsburgh. When I approached him at the door, I told him, "Ron, I'm Joane Roll, your Pittsburgh Chapter President." He said, "Oh, Joane, I'm so glad to meet you and thank you for all you did for me." He then took my hand and led me to meet Betty Hutton. After she placed her hand in mine, she said to me, "Ronald really does have some attractive ladies for his dedicated fans." Ronald just smiled and nodded his head "yes."

He then handed me my admission ticket that he asked for me, and I still own it, as you can see and am glad to share it with you. We shared an enjoyable afternoon talking together. All three of us walked up to the Syria Mosque from the Schenley Hotel. The stage play received favorable reviews for both of them.

It certainly was a memorable day for me. Totally unforgettable because he thanked me for all I did for him and even complimented my loyalty to it all.

Between all the letters I wrote and books I've read, it inspired me to experience creative writings. I feel I was blessed by God in my selection of Ron, not only because of the good actor he was, but because of his development in his political life, and which to him, as a true Christian, he felt it was truly God's purpose for him in his life. He truly felt it was his purpose to serve and improve his fellow man in this country. And, to educate all in the United States that it was in their best interest not to let the government control all the things they needed for a good and more prosperous life.

There were so many times when he wrote me a letter, he sent me a wallet size picture of him. As you can see, it certainly was more than once.

The following pages will give to you an example of "The Reagan Record," a very lengthy report from Zelda Multz, the fan club president, with articles written by different members of Ron's fan club. This copy of "The Reagan Record," the 11th Anniversary Issue, is dated August 15, 1951.

REAGAN RECORD

By RITA BONETTI

11th Anniversary Issue
DEDICATED WITH FOND MEMORIES
TO DIXON, ILLINOIS

THE ONLY OFFICIAL RONALD REAGAN FAN CLUB

Presents

"T H E   R E A G A N   R E C O R D"

HONORARY PRESIDENT: RONALD REAGAN, c/o Warner Bros. Studios
                    Burbank, California

President & Editor: Zelda Multz, 158 Suffolk St., N.Y. 2, N.Y.
Secretary: Lorraine Rutkowski, 167 Colonie St., Albany, N.Y.

DEPARTMENTS

Correspondence: Bonnie Hadland, 1330 Monroe St. N.E. Mpls. Minn.
Pen Pals: Ruth Reiter, 314 So. Chicago Ave., Freeport, Ill.
Publicity: Jane Swadener, 1429 N. Denny, Indianapolis, Ind.
Hobbies: Tim Lowery, Box 136, Tiltonsville, Ohio
Art: Barbara Baxter, Box 106, R.F.D. 3, Old River
                  Road, Valley Falls, Rhode Island
Personality: Anna Blackburn, 427 So. Chicago Ave., Brazil, Ind.

CHAPTERS

Baltimore: Helen Akkas, 2707 St. Paul St., Baltimore, Md.
Canada: Edytha Pieplow, 221 Virginia Ave., Toronto, Ont.
Chicago: Marianne Richter, 5424 W. Madison St., Chicago
Dixon, Ill.   Darlene Shippert, R. R. 4, Dixon, Ill.
England: Ada Fox, 36 The Grange, Bermondsey, London
New York   Marguerite Huebner, 114-46 207th St., St. Albans,
                  Long Island, N.Y.
Philadelphia: Lorraine Makler, 1818 So. 24th St., Phila. 45
Pittsburgh: Joan Roll, 4219 Perrysville Ave., Pittsburgh
San Francisco: Jo Licciardello, 268 Cotter St., San Francisco

ASSOCIATED WITH: International Fan Club League
                  Movie Stars Parade Fan Club Directory
                  Movie Fan Magazine Fan Club Column
                  Movie Spotlight Fan Club Directory
                  United Fan Club
                  Fan Club Publicity

HONORARY MOTHER: Mrs. John E. Reagan

HONORARY MEMBERS: Jane Wyman, Betty Burr, Hup MacArthur,
                  Bette Davis, Jeff Donnell, Humphry Bogart,
                  Jean Steele, James Brown, Arlene Polito,
                  Mrs. Montague Love, Jean Bernhard,
                  Terry Sevigny, Mr. & Mrs. Ben Imhoff,
                  Penny Edwards, Lyle Melvin

* * ** * * ** * * ** * * ** * *

I am the Joan Roll—Pittsburgh mentioned. The next letter was written by Zelda Multz to all the club members and included her announcement of Ronald's visit to his hometown, Dixon, Illinois.

New York, N. Y.

Hello!

Er..is it safe to come in? I mean, you've put away the bats and pitchers and won't throw anything? Golly, you must think I'm one heck of a club prexy delaying the journal for such a long time. Believe me gang - I lost more sleep over this issue than the biggest problem the UN ever faced! (okay - it's a slight exaggeration!) Did you ever know it to fail when you're trying to make a good impression on some special people - only to have things go flooey? There I was, all set to show the folks in Dixon that we had a good club, and a good journal - so I have to get this issue out late! Had the hardest time getting all the Dixon material down on paper - but boy, could I tell it - in about 3 hours, that is! However, I made an attempt. I'm really grateful to you all for being so patient and not belaboring me to "get with it" sooner. Youse is too good to me!

Before going any further, Moms Nelle has asked me to thank you all very much for remembering her at Xmas and other holidays, by sending such lovely cards and gifts. She says she'd love to reciprocate, but knows you all understand that it would be a slight impossibility, as most of her time is spent at the hospitals and sanatoriums for the more unfortunate.

Becuz of the length of this issue, a few of our feature articles have been omitted, but will be included in the next issue, deadline for which is JUNE 30th. Get your material in early!

Of course, the Dixon celebration is still vivid in my mind and is something I'll never forget. I believe Lorraine has more than ably expressed our sentiments about it in her article HOMETOWN, U.S.A. Everyone in Dixon was so good to us and made us feel right at home. As for Dutch - he's everything we expected and more. Put us at our ease immediately and as for Moms Nelle - she is just as sweet as we expected. Didn't think it could be possible, but because he has such a firm grip, Ron's hand swelled up so that he would grimace everytime someone grasped his hand. The nicest compliment Ron could ever receive , but which he didn't hear, came from the friend of an old buddy of Ron's, who said "he isn't puffed up a bit", and that's for sure!

Ron's brother Neil, will be very pleased to learn that a great many of his old friends inquired about him and wondered why he too, hadn't returned home for a visit!

Isn't it swell news to learn that Ron is now 7th in Modern Screen's popularity poll? Let's keep up the good work, gang, and get him up in the number one spot - it shouldn't be too hard! By the way, the May issue of Movie Stars Parade will feature Ron - as will the June issue of Screen Stories featuring THE LAST OUTPOST.

Member Carrie DeHart, along with some friends, is sponsoring gifts to Veterans of the Korean battle, at the Valley Forge Hospital. Anyone wishing to help by contributing either funds or small gifts, will be doing a good deed. Send them to Carrie at 1159 Cotton St., Reading, Pennsylvania.

(1)

More Prexy Chatter

Had the pleasure of seeing and talking to Terry Sevigny again, when she came East for a visit with her folks. Sorry I couldn't see you off for the coast, Terry! Couldn't get out to LaGuardia on time! Also met and had dinner with Ditty Ward and her brother, and had a very nice chat with Louise Warnes, during her visit to town.

Of course, I don't have to mention that I'm somewhat peeved at the fact that we still didn't receive the 75 votes for Ron in Movie Fan Requests Section. I'm very disappointed. Now, I have a serious question - to instigate more club interest - is it necessary to institute a point system? Please let me have your views about this, huh?

Our sincere congratulations to Dutch for being re-elected Prexy of the Screen Actors Guild for a 5th term, and for being among ten of Hollywood's Best Citizens as chosen by a group of columnists.

Some of you have written in to ask about buying snaps that were taken at Dixon - however, as I expect to use many of them in future journals, have deferred their sale. No sense buying the snaps when you'll eventually get them in a future journal.

If you haven't received your membership card and photo from Ron as yet, please be patient, as he has been travelling quite a bit, and most likely, has a lot of back mail to catch up with.

And speaking of mail - please continue to bear with me. I'm slowly getting some of my mail done, and perhaps by the end of 1951, I'll be caught up with 1950's mail!

By the way, I sure hope that those of you whose membership expires with this issue, will renew once again. We're glad to have you with us - and again, if you haven't received all 3 journals due you under your membership (if it expires with this issue), let me know so my records can be marked accordingly.

Isn't the cover sketch wonderful? I'm certainly grateful to Rita Bonetti for drawing the photo of Ronnie and also for having it lithographed and "donating" it to the club. Rita is prexy of the Danny Scholl Fan Club - with wonderful journals. Contact her at 2145 So. 13th Street, Philadelphia, Pa. if you are interested.

Once again - we have no index for this issue - not enough room. Chapter doings seem to be waning - hope it's just spring fever. Names and addresses of chapter prexies are always listed, so if you know of a chapter in your vicinity, contact the gal in charge. If you want a biography of Ron - contact Bonnie Hadland, 1330 Monroe St. N.E., Minneapolis, Minn. Enclose a stamped envelope.

Of course, it goes without saying that the people of Dixon have our everlasting gratitude for making our sojurn in their wonderful town something to remember always - and that wonderful gang at the C. of C. - what more can we say, after we've said you're WONDERFUL! Till the next issue then -

P.S. The club gifted Ron with a leather travelling case (fitted) for his birthday.

Devotedly,

Zelda

(2)

You can see we were all very busy fans (almost as busy as Ronald was); dedicated and loyal to all the events in Ronald's life.

The next page shows Ronald's written response to his hometown visit in Dixon, Illinois, with his mother, Moms Nelle, with him, being honored by all the hometown natives at the "Indian Summer Days" event. When he wrote their letter for his "Reagan Record," he was commenting and telling everyone about the events that were happening at that time.

Typical of Ronald, giving thanks and praise to Zelda Murtz for her loyal, active presidency. Maureen and Mike are two of his children to whom he was referring.

And then thanks from Ron for the gift sent for his birthday with his signature.

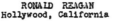

RONALD REAGAN
Hollywood, California

Dear Friends:

If this letter gets a little hurried, you'll have to forgive me, but I think I've been on a "merry-go-round" for quite awhile.

In August, I hit the road for appearances with the opening of "Louisa" and wound up in Dixon, for a very wonderful homecoming celebration, which you've probably already read about. The only thing I didn't do for four weeks, was sleep. Upon my return to California, I had one day to send my laundry out and then reported to Universal for a picture called "Bedtime For Bonzo".

You'll have to see this - my co-stars are Diana Lynn (who is really great) and a five year old chimpanzee who steals every scene. I haven't seen the results yet, but word is getting around that it is a very fine picture.

This one ended, and I had one day (to pick up my laundry) and left for Arizona with Rhonda Fleming, Bill Williams, Noah Berry, Jr., Hugh Beaumont and, of course, "Tar Baby", to do one called "The Last Outpost". Keep your fingers crossed on this one. At last, I got my "outdoor" picture, and I'm very anxious for it to be okay. We licked the Indians, the Union forces and got the girl - all in technicolor!

It doesn't seem possible that the club is having it's 11th anniversary, but it is, thanks to you - and to Zelda, for stepping in when Arlene and Terry had to give it up, and what a fine Prexy you've turned out to be. I take my hat off to you.

Now, Maureen and Mike are waiting for a trip to the ranch, so I'll have to close, or get burned at the stake.

By the way, let me say the journal was mighty fine.

Best always,

Ronnie

AN EXTRA NOTE FROM RONNIE!

Dear Friends:

This is just a "quickie" to tell you how much I appreciated the beautiful gift and book of greetings on my birthday. The travelling case is good looking enough to make me hope my suitcase falls open in a crowd sometime, so I can show it off. Incidentally, any gift for travel seems very appropriate these days. I've been on the road so much, I feel like a tourist just passing through California, when I'm home.

As for the book of greetings - it goes without saying what that means to me, and will in days to come. Again, my heartfelt thanks to all of you and best wishes always.

Sincerely,

Ronnie

(3)

Here on the following pages is the full report of "Hometown, USA" by Lorraine Makler (who is now Lorraine Wagner). There is a very talented report of the hometown event for Ronald with pictures taken at the event. One was Ronald with Lorraine, the second was Moms Nelle, Ronald and Mrs. Walgreen.

Ron and Lorraine

Moms Nelle, Ronald and Mrs. Walgreen

HOMETOWN, U.S.A.
By...Lorraine Makler

Dixon, Illinois is the kind of wonderful community that has given
our United States the renowned reputation of which it has boasted
these many years, for actually Dixon is _more_ than just a town, it's
a symbol of the friendship and the spirit of a greaty country and
of the truly fine citizens who are its lifeblood - the very pulse
of our nation!

Knowing that Dixon is Ronnie's hometown is an establishment of the
fact that it's citizenry is a cross-section of America's finest;
for when these people opened to us their hands and their hearts and
their homes with no more provocation than just that Zelda and I had
asked to join their celebration in honor of thier "DUTCH", it was
the kind of reception that endeared to us the American way of life,
a perspective which one sometimes has difficulty holding in the
hustle and bustle of big city life. Truthfully, the warmth of their
welcome and the friendship which we eagerly accepted will remain
engraved in our hearts a lifetime!!!

INJUN SUMMER DAYS is an annual August event and each summer the
town's 14,000 plan feverishly to top the preceeding year's record
for noteworthy entertainment and interest - and without a doubt,
they certainly achieved an all-time high this thrilling summer
of 1950.

To Dixon's happy throngs, "DUTCH" was more than just the "local
boy making good," because their keen memories could remember the
lanky youngster who devilishly frightened girls into believing
there were water rats by throwing rocks in the river when he was
eager to end his daily lifeguard chores at Lowell Beach and to return to town for that 'date'; and they remembered the high school
boy who loved dramatics, and they remembered how much a-part of him
were the football games and the swimming contests he won and just
all kinds of athletics, and they remembered the friendly "Hi" and
the irresistible smile..and they just loved Hollywood's
Ronald Reagan'!.!

True, Dixon would always remember him as "Dutch", just the way he
wanted it, but they missed him, and for 9 years, Ronnie kept himself so busy becoming an undeniably fine actor and one of Hollywood's most loved and respected citizens that he too was forced to
bask in just the thoughts of his old friends and the places he knew
to well. Ronnie grew up in Dixon and it's not easy to forget sur-
roundings as engraved as Dixon's were in that sponge-like memory

(continued on next page)

Hometown, U.S.A. (continued from page 21)

of his, and the eagerness to return to the scene where his really outstanding character was effectively developed and molded was offset only by the force of inertia which fooled him into believing that his friends were not as anxious to see him as he was to swap old yarns with them!!!

Yeah, so disinterested were they that Ed Lawton, an officer of Dixon's Chamber of Commerce, and an old school chum of Ron's, joined forces with Lyle Melvin, first Vice Prexy of the C. of C. and as early as February, 1950, traveled all the way to Los Angeles to ask Dutch to become the HONOR GUEST at the "RONALD REAGAN INJUN SUMMER DAYS" festivities from August 20 to 23! You can bet that this town, with the enormous heart, didn't forget Moms Nelle, either, for Dutch's mother was held as high in esteem as her famous son and Dixon saw to it that both shared "billing" in a series of hectic, but heart-warming and tear-provoking activities.

Ron and Moms Nelle barely had time to sleep - but they were home among the people who missed them and loved them with the kind of ageless affection and devotion which can come only with the years and with the memories they had shared.

In the American tradition, it is to the real "big towns" like Dixon to which we owe an eternal debt of gratitude for giving us the opportunity of developing the minds and personalities of our children into something beneficial to world wide understanding! With all due respect and admiration to the people of Dixon, thanks from the very bottom of our hearts - we salute you and admire you!!

DIXON -- DIXON -- DIXON -- DIXON -- DIXON -- DIXON -- DIXON -- DIXON

GUEST OF HONOR
By..Edgar A. Guest

He looked about the table with a
   twinkle none could miss
Then said: "I want to tell you I
   have always hoped for this.
Down the years I've often
   wondered if the day would ever be
When those I've known and worked with
   would a party give for me.
Man works for fame and fortune but
   there's more to be desired
For a man may long for friendship
   when his fortune is acquired.
When his comrades meet to praise
   him, it is music to his ears,
And no reward is greater for the
   labor of his years.
It is this that I have hoped for
   It is this I've tried to win,
The faith of all my fellows when
   the resting days begin.
Just a party such as this one;
   friends who still believe in me
This I say is true achievement;
   this is man's best victory."

Contributed by Marguerite Huebner, who thought this would be a perfect dedication for the banquet held in Ron's honor in Dixon.
(22)

DATA FROM DIXON   By..Dorothy for Darlene Shippert

"Keeping Up With Nelle" (is quite a job)

Immediately following the "Injun Summer" doings, as you know, Moms
Nelle went along with our Dutch to the Tampico celebration. From an
"on-the-spot" broadcast "Folks in Tampico are out full-force to
show the beloved Reagans how much they appreciate them." Two old
fellows standing near me, as Ronald and Moms Nelle rode by in the
parade, smiling and waving, were commenting as follows:

One said, "Well sir, Nellie just hasn't changed a bit". And then
the other fellow said, "and you know - according to what I hear,
her boys have turned out right good. Now, you take this boy, Ronnie-
just as common a feller as you could ask fer." Rubbing his chin re-
flectively, "You know - Hollywood must not be so bad as it's painted
mebbe, huh?" (to which we may add fervently, Amen).

Upon Mrs. Reagan's return to Dixon, old friends had a huge old-
fashioned "Scramble-Picnic" for "Our Nelle". It was to be at Lowell
Park (where Ron was life guard), but due to rainy weather, it was
held in the Christian Church Parlors - more than a hundred people -
and in Nelle's own words, "The most delicious variety of foods you
can imagine!" Pictures were taken of the bountifully-laden tables;
and of the various groups of friends. It was completely informal as
in yester-years. A spontaneous program of Readings and Musical
numbers (induced by the oft-repeated "remember whens..." and featured our dear friends and classmates of years gone by..."Genie"
Straw; Mary Hintz Morrel, and Ora Floto Tice, and the Mother and
Daughter duet, Dorothy and Darlene Shippert, and others...all helped
to "roll back the years to give Nelle a picnic she "will never
forget"! Her inspirational talk was something the crowd will
remember as the "high spot" of her visit.

Mrs. Reagan stayed at the home of her very dear old friends, Mr.
and Mrs. Emory Countryman, between her fast rounds of activities.
From there, she visited the Convalescent patients in the Mansion
Nursing Home and K.S.B. Public Hospital, several times; also the
County Jail...to give cheer and encouragement to the unfortunate,
in her dear and well-remembered way.

After a trip to see relatives at Springfield and at Morrison,
Illinois; (and I believe there was also a return to Tampico for a
picnic)...she returned to Dixon for a scheduled appointment to
visit the Lee County Nursing Home, September 12. All movable
patients were assembled in the Recreation Room for the program as
follows; vocal duets by Dorothy and Darlene Shippert, accompanied
by Ethel Shippert, who also played piano solos; several accordian
numbers by Stephen Berei, Jr. (aged 9 years and one of our two
youngest R.R.F.C. Dixon members) and a talk by our Nelle, on the
Power of Prayer. Ethel and Stephen then went to other engagements,
and Nelle and "The Girls" went upstairs to tour the rooms of the
bedfast patients. A personal visit at each bedside - a little gift
of candy while the "Girls" sang from strategic points in the halls.

(continued on next page)

Data From Dixon (continued from page 23)

While in Dixon, Mr. and Mrs. Winston McReynolds and family were proud to entertain Nelle Reagon with a delicious turkey dinner!

Nelle spent her last evening in Dixon with her friends, Mr. and Mrs. J. Sipe, who then took her to Chicago where she visited a nephew while awaiting a train reservation for California. She had to wait almost ten days, during which time I hope she rested; but knowing Nelle, I imagine she found many hospitals to visit!......

The following which was in Dorothy's letter to me was so impressive, I decided to include it below:

"Let me go on record here as saying it was with some reluctance and hesitation, that I pondered whether to divulge some of these items for fear of embarrassing Ronald and Moms Nelle with our obvious tributes to their fine characters. I happen to know that they do not do these things "for the plaudits of man," but as Nelle has said to me, 'These are the things we do for our Heavenly Father, don't you know?' Soo -- my hesitation, till I remembered that this is a publication which goes to their ardent friends and best-wishers (not the type of readers who are looking for 'dirt'. Let me also go on record as sincerely believing that it is such as Dutch, with friends among Jewish, Catholic and Protestant; his friends being chosen regardless of color of skin; his genuine dislike of class distinctions, and a complete freedom from race prejudice - and with the courage of his convictions, will inevitably rise to great heights."

Editor's Note: The Dixon chapter held its first meeting in January and it was very successful, what with the lucky people getting a chance to see home movies of the celebration, thanks to Don Stauffer, Gene Lebre and Winston McReynolds, who pooled their films - plus an added attraction of a film taken in 1942 when Dutch visited Dixon along with his Mom and a group of other stars. Cooperation came too, from the Dixon Evening Telegraph who inserted the notice in one of their editions, reminding the members of the meeting! You don't know how lucky you folks are!!

* * * * * * * *

WHEN WAS THE LAST TIME YOU WROTE TO RONALD REAGAN? DO IT AGAIN, NOW!

RON, MOMS NELLE and
MRS. CHARLES WALGREEN
at "Hazelwood"

(24)

You can tell what active, talented personalities were giving loyal and high tribute to Ronald Reagan. I enjoyed immensely my years in his fan club and was delighted with the fact that Ronald Reagan turned out to be the sensitive, hard-working man he is. He was as dedicated and loyal to us as we were to him.

THREE

Personal Letters and Autographed Pictures

IN 1960 I experienced a devastating fire in the apartment where my family was living. Almost everything we owned was destroyed in the fire.

I did lose many personal letters and cards from Ronald, but I felt a miracle from God saved the ones I will now share with you. I am sure you will notice the scorch marks on some of the letters and cards. But most of them clearly hold Ron's own handwriting.

When I joined his fan club and started writing Ronald twice a month, he answered me briefly. Then, later, these grew into more lengthy messages and information about him and the fan club activities. Many of the letters were "thank you" ones from him.

The first card was signed and autographed by him on May 6, 1948.

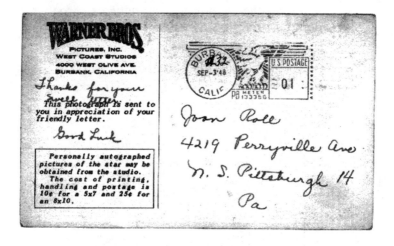

The second card was sent, as you can see, in September, 1948. From May until September, he was giving all his time to the SAG.

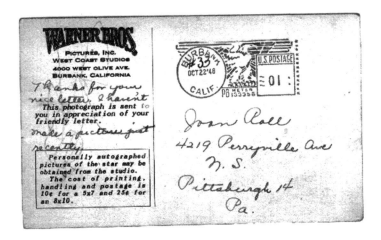

Third card—He was still so busy negotiating with SAG that he did not even have time to start his next movie. October 22, 1948.

Wallet-sized picture

Ronald Reagan
Warner Bros. Studios
Burbank, California

Dear Joan : - Now I hope you get this letter O-K, 'cause I'm writing one, as you see, if you get it.

And the only picture I could find that you might be able to use in your wallet is herein enclosed, perhaps I can do better some other time if I ever get a chance to have some snaps taken.

Well, I am crossing the Ocean in a few weeks, going to England to make a picture, this is something I've dreamed of, ever since I signed up with Warner Bros. and now that dream _is_ coming true, oh! Boy!

Am mighty busy getting every thing in order here before I go, and have a Board meeting in about three quarters of an hour so this must be short, but never-the-less

November 2 letter

Ronald Reagan
Warner Bros. Studios
Burbank, California

it is a letter, isn't it ??

Always keep fighting for us June, "atta girl." I appreciate your interest and who knows, maybe everything will end right before June comes, my fingers are crossed, and the old saying you know "Absence makes the heart grow fonder," maybe June will realize "I'm her man."

You forgot to enclose the picture so I would know if you were "white or black," as you wrote in your letter.

My mail will still be picked up at Warner Bros. Studio Burbank, so hope you'll remember to enclose it the next. Most Sincerely

Ronald

The next letter, written to me from Ron, is one of my most prized possessions. He was sharing his feelings with me about the end of his marriage to Jane Wyman. As he sent me a wallet-sized picture that is here for you to see, I sent one of me to him. The date was November 2, 1948. He was planning to sail to England to star in *The Hasty Heart*.

Then, on November 10, 1948, I received this written card from him, hoping I received his last letter and picture he sent to me. I received all his mail, but acting as a dedicated fan, I kept writing to him several times a month and, noticeably, he did not have the time to answer them all. But he did want my assurance that I was receiving the ones he wrote me. He also sent this autographed picture to me. He then left for England aboard the *S.S. Britannica*, to star in his very good film, *The Hasty Heart*. On the back of this picture, he thanked me for sending him a picture of me, which he had requested of me.

The written card dated September 22, 1949, is one of my favorite replies from him. He was still on crutches but remembered working hard for the SAG. The charity work he is congratulating us for refers to the dance we held in his name. Rita Ermell, one of the members of his fan club at that time, helped me a lot with all the details and later gave the money received to "shut-in" children in that area. As you can see, he is again telling me about the charitable work his mother, Moms Nelle, was doing. He then signed the card on the right side. Again, he was telling me not to believe everything I read about him from the reporters on his activities. That's why I asked him after reading he was wanted for a Broadway play and he said "Don't believe all you read."

May 22, 1949 letter

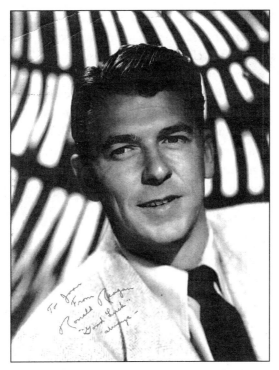

Autographed 8 x 10

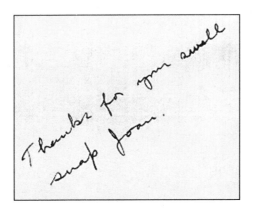

The next letter was written by him on May 22, 1949.

He did send me my new signed membership card which you read in the first chapter. He was assuring me he took care of all his letters from his fans, and as I told everyone, the only one that helped him from time to time was his sister-in-law. Bessie and his Moms Nelle occasionally wrote to his fans. Like I told you, they always signed their names, not his.

The grandfather he is referring to was Rose Marie Obermier's, a fan club member, one who wrote him regularly. He sent me this autographed picture shortly after sending me these letters.

8 - 7th 49

Dear Joan : This letter should
have been written long ago, for
I did get the swell handkerchiefs —
both of them, but was slow about
thanking you, and "then came the
accident", "well - it had to be postponed
for "painful" reasons, but the old broken
leg is coming through fine so hope
to be out of hospital soon, and then
on crutches, have been flat on my
back for seven weeks, to-day, and a
few more weeks to go, before they
get me on the crutches.

Its a bit hard to write in the
position I'm in, so will say many
thanks again, and Best wishes always.

Ronnie —

August 7, 1949 letter

The next letter, dated August 7, 1949, was written to me while Ron was in the hospital after shattering his leg while playing a charity baseball game. But the thoughtful man was apologizing for not writing me before it all happened. He was still in the hospital at the time and spent many months on crutches after being flat on his back for several months in leg traction.

In the early 1950s, he signed a contract with General Electric to appear as their MC on their show. He not only MC'd every show, he starred in some of them. GE developed a lecturing tour to all the different GE plants for their employees.

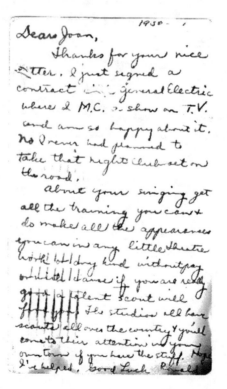

From 1950s, when he signed up with G.E. Theatre

He wrote me this handwritten card when he signed on the GE and was still president of the SAG. Ronald was always a very hard-working man; he had to be, to do all he did for his career, as well as for his family and his ranch maintenance.

He just returned from putting on a very successful night-club act and I asked him if he ever thought of taking it on the road. And, as you can read, he never planned on that. It was a good decision for him because he did sign up with GE and went on tour with them. At this time I was taking piano and singing lessons and asked him how to promote myself as a singer. As you can read, he told me the right action to take to start it all.

Ronald Reagan
Warner Bros. Studios
Burbank, California

Dear Joan: I dont know if I ever thanked you for my swell Christmas present, I guess a little bird must have told you I was getting pretty low on "Hankies," and you have sent them at other times too, for which I am most grateful.

Oh! Yes, and I want you to know how I appreciate your letters, I read and enjoy them even though I dont get a chance to write very often my self and its swell of you to be so understanding about it. The work you are doing in the name of the club is very fine, and please dont over work I wouldn't want you to get ill on account of trying to do so much. Now about the Radio deal that you thought of- it would be fine, but just couldn't be done, for at the present my movie contracts prevent

March 11, 1950 letter

me accepting any thing but occasional guest programs. When they put on a charity program, and all we Stars were contacted to take part I of course, consented, and later was told by the Big bosses, I could not appear in this show. well the out-come of all this — brought me many letters from Fans who wrote to tell me I was getting like a lot of the stars; let folk believe I would appear, and not show up, because I had gone Hollywood, and felt myself to big a star to have to do simple things to please the people any more. I feel pretty badly about it, because as "God is my witness" I love nothing better than to give my services to raise money for all the things the movie needed to help less unfortunate, and yet I have no way of letting the public know how wrong they are in judging me such a heel. Well Joan here I've been crying on your shoulder, pardon me for taking the privilege. I imagine there are a lot more letters from you among all the unopened letters I have, and I'll be reading them believe me.

Always my best & my thanks for your loyalty to you & the old. Rudell —

The letter sent on March 11, 1950, is another good example of Ron's volunteering his services to humanitarian, charitable interests. When prevented from appearing on a charity
broadcast show by his Warner Brothers Studio bosses, he
received a lot of negative letters from fans that did not really
know his charitable ways. As you can read, he was very upset
about that. He knew I understood what happened and he
asked for pardon for "crying on [my] shoulder" about the situation. He also knew I promoted him as a loving, God-
inspired humanitarian. The handkerchiefs he refers to at the
beginning of the letter were for his birthday on February 6.
He thanked me many times for my loyalty to him.

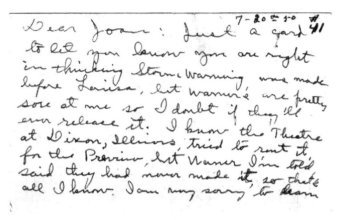

July 20, 1950 card

His next written card to me, on July 20, 1950, referred to his continuous problem at that time with Warner Brothers. They were so upset with him because he was giving much time to serving the SAG, as well as GE Theater. Warner Brothers finally released *Storm Warning* and it received favorable reviews. You will find out more about it in the "Movies" chapter.

August 29, 1953 card

When I experienced the total wipeout of my possessions due to the fire in my apartment, I lost several of Ron's letters and personal pictures. So, the next one I saved is dated August 29, 1953—a card giving me information about him and his family.

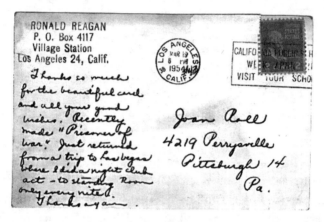

March 19, 1954 card

The next one saved was March 19, 1954, thanking me again for his birthday gift and informing me that he had just returned from Las Vegas, where he put on a very successful nightclub act that received great critic reviews.

Although you may notice the scorch marks on the next letter, dated January 11, 1955, I felt it was worth saving because Ronald was thanking me for the gift I sent to him and Nancy. And, again, he tells me about his hard-working, time-consuming schedule.

Dear Joan,

You probably think we are a fine pair never having acknowledged your beautiful handkerchiefs. Nancy is as pleased as I am and thinks here really very lovely as I do. You were a very nice person to remember us when you no doubt have many gifts to buy in your own family.

I have been really working like a demon of late what with my TV show, my trips back and forth across the country to say nothing of all my activities right here.

We got a kick out of Patricia Ann this Xmas. She enjoyed the gifts more than the wrappings this year. She's real chubby and is a big girl for only two.

Thank you again Joan and we both hope the New Year year brings all good things to you.

Ronald

January 11, 1955 letter

Patricia Ann was only two years old at that time and they both were really enjoying her at that age.

The next handwritten card I have from Ron is marked March 8, 1956, and may be hard for you to read due to the moisture during the fire. Talking about his GE trips, Ron actually had little to say about them. "GE plans each day for me and although it's work, I enjoy it. Moms Nelle is OK. Am still enjoying the ranch. Good luck—Ronald."

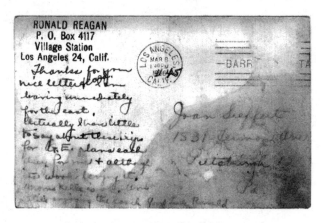

March 8, 1956 card

I was asking about his mom because she developed painful arthritis and was heading towards senility.

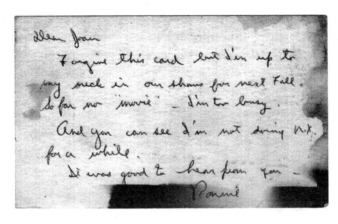

August 16, 1956 card

The written card of August 16, 1956, was very brief, but he at least took the time to answer my letters as best he could. GE tours were costing him all his time on the road.

December 7, 1956 card

Then came his written message of December 7, 1956. He finally allowed himself the time to star in another movie, this time with his wife, Nancy Davis. They were both on location filming *Hellcats of the Navy*.

RONALD REAGAN

Dec. 31

Dear Joan

Just a line to thank you for your very handsome Xmas gift. (Even if it is Westinghouse) You really shouldn't have done it but even so Nancy & I are very grateful and have a place all picked out for it. We won't let G.E. know but we are already enjoying it.

Again our thanks & very best wishes for a Happy New Year —

Best Regards

Ronnie

December 31, 1956 letter

At the time I received this next letter from Ron, I was working as a bookkeeping clerk at Westinghouse Electric on the north side in Pittsburgh, Pennsylvania. And even though I knew Ronald was working for GE (General Electric) at the time, I sent him and Nancy a radio entertainment system I had received at a bargain price while working at Westinghouse. As you can read, they did enjoy it. I sent the gift before Christmas and his answer was dated December 31, 1956.

The next prized letter I received was from his mother, Moms Nelle, dated May 15, 1956. I had personally written her six times and received answers from her, most of them lost in my home fire.

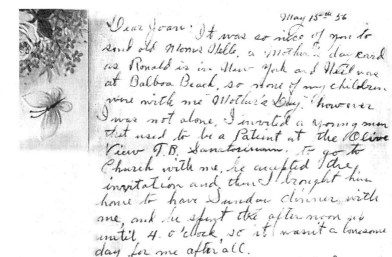

get to see much of them, but they
do call me by Phone so it's nice to
hear their dear voices.

Yes Joan dear I received your letter
telling me of your marriage, but I
don't remember answering that letter, there
was some sickness I had, that the doctor said
I must not write, for when I tried to, my
head would begin to ache so I could not
stand it. The 23rd of Feb. on my way from
visiting Olive View, a young man struck
my car head on and smashed it up badly
my car was standing still for the stop
sign, had I been moving I think I
would have been killed, as it was I
was badly injured, but am beginning

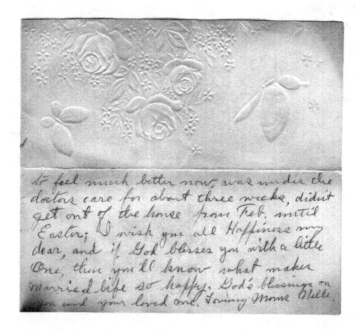

to feel much better now, was under the
doctors care for about three weeks, didn't
get out of the house from Feb. until
Easter; I wish you all Happiness my
dear, and if God blesses you with a little
One, then you'll know what makes
married life so happy. God's blessings on
you and your loved One. Loving Mame Nelle.

I just sent her a Mother's Day card with a letter in it. And her answer to my letter will inform you of the charitable volunteer she was. Moms Nelle, at this time, was a steady volunteer at the Olivia View TB Sanitarium. She even took the patients along with her to different places. This letter was after she was involved in an automobile accident and she was apologizing for not answering my last letter. As you can read, she was sending me God's blessings on my recent marriage. I was extremely fond of this lovable lady. She experienced not only the automobile accident, but later developed arthritis, which gave her quite a lot of pain. As she grew older, she started getting senile and required special care.

I still feel and know that Ronald acquired his charitable, loving, humanitarian ways directly from her, even though Ronald developed larger ones than she could give—but the Christian approach to all his efforts started from Nelle.

January 1957 card

Ronald sent this next card to me in January 1957, thanking me for the handkerchiefs I sent him and Nancy. I did watch the GE show on Christmas night. And I enjoyed the family situation, even though Patti was ill with mumps that kept her from appearing on the television telecast on Christmas day.

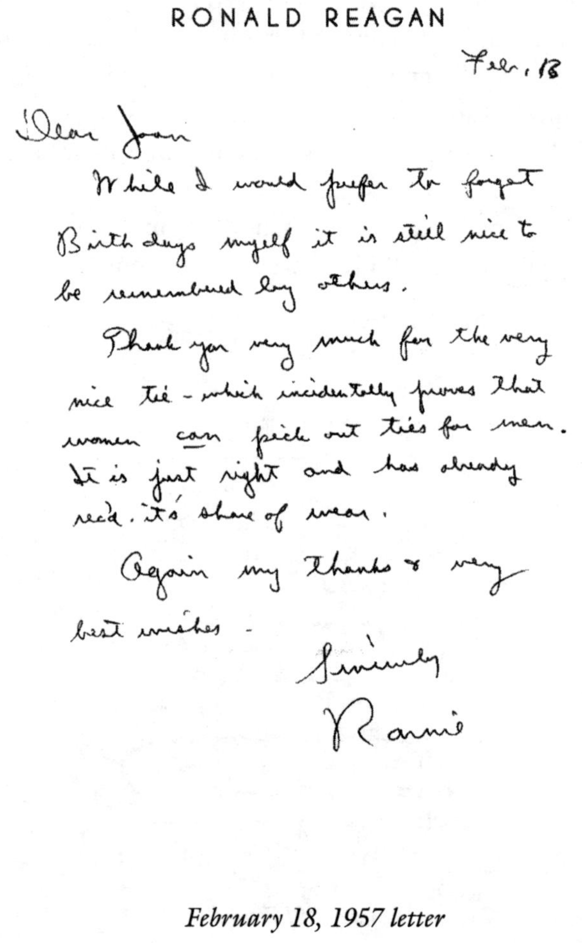

RONALD REAGAN

Feb, 18

Dear Joan

While I would prefer to forget Birthdays myself it is still nice to be remembered by others.

Thank you very much for the very nice tie – which incidentally proves that women _can_ pick out ties for men. It is just right and has already rec'd. it's share of wear.

Again my thanks & very best wishes –

Sincerely

Ronnie

February 18, 1957 letter

His next letter to me thanked me for the tie I sent him for his birthday, February 6th. Moms Nelle also wrote me a note telling me how she liked my choice of a tie for her Ronald. The letter was dated February 18, 1957.

Drake Hotel card dated June 8, 1957

The written card showing the Drake Hotel Ron sent me telling me he was on the road again doing GE lecture tours. Zelda Multz, at that time president of the Ronald Reagan Fan Club, is the one he told me to give his best to. I planned to go to New York at that time, so I did visit and exchange a lot of fan club activities with her. This one was dated June 8, 1957. He also talked about having to be away from his ranch and his horses.

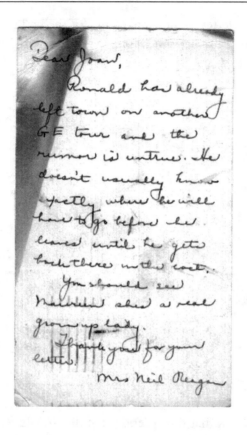

Card from Mrs. Neil Reagan, dated October 14, 1957

October 14, 1957, Ronald was so busy on his GE tours that his sister-in-law, Bessie Reagan, wrote me in answer to my letters to him. Maureen, Ron's daughter, was the one she was telling me about. As you can see, the signed it Mrs. Neil Reagan, Ronald's brother's wife. Bessie was a very thoughtful lady when she took the time to help Ronald with his mail, but always signed her name, not his.

RONALD REAGAN
PACIFIC PALISADES, CALIFORNIA

Aug. 13.

Dear Joan

First of all let me say I'm happy any time some one "kicks back" at a critic. We've found that critics never like the shows the people like and when the critics do like one the audience rarely does. For example our "David & Goliath" story which she panned was one of our best liked programs and literally hundreds of churches have asked for copies of the script which unfortunately we can't send them because of authors legal rights etc

Now about the gift — you really surprised me because that letter was written a long time ago. It is true we've had this experience before with our little country sub-station. Anyway you didn't get my letter so let me say now thanks very much it was a wonderful & certainly useful gift.

Again thanks + Best Regards

Ronnie

August 13, 1958 letter

Ronald's letter dated August 13, 1958, was talking about a special drama he did on David and Goliath. The kickback he is referring to came from me. Critics at that time did not give good reviews of the play, even though it and the actors were all very good. All the churches wanted copies, but the authors would not allow him to give any copies. He also had trouble with mail reaching his country substation at the time.

June 7

Dear Joan

Just returned from another several weeks on the road for G.E. and found your letters waiting. Had to delay answering while Ronald Prescott Reagan was born.

I know I'm a poor correspondent but hope you'll understand that my life isn't exactly my own in this TV whirl. Not only is there the extensive traveling but my home hours are filled with almost constant story & script reading which can't be put off lest some one else grab a story away from us.

It was good to hear from you and to know how well everything is going. I know how happy you must be.

Best Regards

Ronnie

P.S. The mail address is only because that is more convenient for me in handling mail than it would be at home.

June 7, 1958 letter

The letter he sent me dated June 7, 1958, was written right after he and Nancy had their son, Ronald Prescott, nicknamed "Skipper." In my letter to him, I told him about adopting my first son, Paul. That is what he is referring to when he was telling me, I told him I was very happy about the adoption and I was happy. He knew that kind of happiness, because if you will remember, he also adopted a son while married to Jane Wyman. His name is Michael.

Nancy had Ronald Prescott by cesarean section. Ronald was quite relieved that Nancy turned out well with it all.

RONALD REAGAN
PACIFIC PALISADES, CALIFORNIA

Jan, 2

Dear Joan

Just returned from Pasadena where we've been for a few days preparing to do yesterdays TV broadcast of the Rose parade. When we arrived home last night I found your gift awaiting me. It's a beautiful tie and I'm very grateful to you. It was kind and thoughtful of you to send it. Please accept my thanks and my very best wishes for the coming year.

Best Regards
Sincerly
Ronald

January 2, 1959 letter

January 2, 1960, Ronald MC'd a Rose Bowl Parade on television before he returned and wrote this letter acknowledging my Christmas gift to him. I preferred to send him ties because he was always grateful for my selections.

Feb. 2

Dear Joan

I'm sorry to be so late in writing to thank you for the gift but as usual G.E. has had me in & out of town several times.

At any rate thank you very much for all of us. Our "spirited steed" is already on display at the ranch where we thought he'd be more at home than in city life.

Again our thanks & very best regards

Sincerely
Ronnie

February 2, 1960 letter

The next letter, dated February 2, 1960, was handwritten to me following my early-sent birthday gift to him. The gift this time was a beautiful black "spirited steed horse." It was a Black Ebony statue that he put on display at his ranch home. And he was acknowledging my intentions of including Nancy when I sent the gift.

The next letters you will read are from Bessie Reagan because of Ronald's busy work schedule with GE Tours. All are from the 1960s.

1960

Dear Joan,

Thanks so much for your very nice letter. Ronald has been gone on one of his long G E Tour and returns this week.

First of all Mrs Reagan is so well physically but mentally has become quite senile and we all feel so sorry. We have a lady living with her to take care of her at present.

Maureen lives in Washington DC at present and is working, Mike is with Ronald and Nancy – he is such a nice boy. Patty has grown like a weed and baby Ronald just two months like yours into everything – talks a blue streak and is quite a "guy". Of course Ronald doesn't get to go to the ranch nearly so much as he would like but he takes every

1960 letter from Bessie Reagan

opportunity he can get.

Am so sorry to hear about Zelda's mother — hope everything is ok by now. I lost my own Mother at the end of Jan. and its really tough parting with one parent.

I do hope you are well and happy as both Neil and I are. Glad you understand that Ronald does have lots of responsibilities & is so busy and although he hears & reads lots of his mail doesn't always have time to answer it.

Good luck to you all

Sincerely

Bessie Reagan

Bessie Reagan was keeping me informed about all Ron's family activities and the health care situation involving his mother, Moms Nelle. I know you read before about Moms Nelle's health problems. In this letter she's describing Ronald and Nancy's family progress. As you can see, she signed her own name.

Bessie wrote me another answer to my letters in the following.

1960

Dear Joan,

I'm so sorry Ronald failed to answer your Xmas gift it must have been a complete oversight. He received the jewel box and liked it very much. He's gone again on another tour and has been so busy.

That fire was really destructive on the ranch. It burned one barn and part of another, all the chickens, fence posts he had worked so hard to put in himself. Of course it burned off all the trees, grass etc. He felt so badly over it all.

You should see how much Patti has grown she's so big and do you know that baby Ronald looks exactly like Patti did at the same age. In fact when little Ronald was real tiny you could not have told he + Patti apart.

I'm terribly sorry to tell you that Ronald's mother is not well. She has become

so senile that it is necessary to have
someone stay with her all the time. It is
so too bad for she was so good and did so
much for others.

I do hope you will forgive him
& I'll be sure to have him write when
he gets back if he has a minute.

Nice to hear about your family.

Good luck and thanks for
writing

Bessie Reagan

In her next letter to me, she was telling me about the fire Ronald had on his ranch that ruined a lot of his property.

He wrote me a thank-you note after he returned from his GE tour at that time. And Bessie again gives me the report about Moms Nelle's senile condition, noting how sorry she was because Moms Nelle did so much for others. This letter is an answer to one I had sent to her.

What really makes me feel sad is knowing that Ronald is now suffering from Alzheimer's and needs constant care. Nancy has been so supportive of Ronald in every event in his life and now she is equally loyal to him in helping to take care of him with this mental illness. I hope and pray God will take care of both Nancy and Ronald.

RONALD REAGAN
PACIFIC PALISADES

November 7, 1962

Mrs. Joan Sieffert
4219 Perrysville Avenue
Pittsburgh 14, Penna.

Dear Joan,

This is a very late answer to your letter but there was some delay in its reaching me due in part to the fact that Ive been in and out of town a great deal.

I want to thank you for your expression of sympathy.   I'm sure you would want to know that in a way it was for the best, and that there was no pain or distress.

You ask me about my plans.   Right now they are somewhat up in the air.   I am hopeful the future may include a picture, and then later on possibly something in television.

Best regards.

Sincerely,

Ronald Reagan

November 7, 1962 letter

The last letter, typewritten by Bessie and signed by Ron on November 7, 1962, was the answer to my sympathy card sent to them after Moms Nelle passed away to her heavenly home. Ronald felt it was a blessing to Moms Nelle, relieving her of all her stress.

You can now see the last autographed picture he sent me.

From reading all my personal letters and cards, you can now see why I know that Ronald Reagan is a true humanitarian.

FOUR

Ronald Reagan's Movie Life and Movie Scene Pictures

RONALD SIGNED HIS contract with Warner Brothers[10] in 1937. For a few months he starred in his first movie, *Love is On the Air*, with Jane Travis.

His second movie right after that was *Sergeant Murphy*, where he played the part of a Cavalryman.

In his third movie, *Submarine D-1*, about a navy flier, his co-star was Pat O'Brien. Ron and Pat O'Brien became good friends and co-starred in his coming movies. Their film made Ronald the Earl Flynn of the "B" movies, according to the critics and reviewers of the film. In those days, there were many "B"-type movies made beside the "A" movies. The"B" movies were made with a much lower budget than the "A" movies and never received the audience attention approval. But it did give Ronald good experience that led him to the "A"-type movies that followed.

---

[10] Hubler. Details given of the films he made.

19. MAUREEN ELIZABETH REAGAN was born in 1941. The expected football player turned out to be a young lady who, though called Monkeypuss by her old man, is really his pride and joy.

20. ON LOCATION for *Juke Girl* with Ann Sheridan. Note the rare glimpse of his glasses. He wears contact lens while working.

21. SERGEANT Craig Reynolds (Marines and ex-Warners') visited Lieut. Reagan, Cavalry Reserve, who'd just been called up.

22. LIEUT. REAGAN with his mother Nell and 15-month-old daughter, Monkeypuss, prior to his departure for active duty with the Army at Oakland.

23. CAPTAIN REAGAN, with Mrs. Reagan, at *This Is The Army* premiere. Now in Air Corps, this was his first picture since 1942.

24. OUT OF SERVICE sign on the ancient jalopy meant just that as Wayne Morris, Harry Lewis, Gig Young, Ronald were given welcome-back studio party.

RAKE IN TIME, saves poppa of work. Reagan Proverbs. ht) Newcomer, Michael Reaadopted member of family.

28. NEW HEAD of powerful Screen Actors Guild stepping with Oscar-winning are so-o proud of

MILESTONES in the MOVIE LIFE of RONALD REAGAN

1. LOVE IS ON THE AIR, 1937. His first was a B.

2. ACCIDENTS WILL HAPPEN, 1938. Gloria Blondell shared this B.

3. DARK VICTORY, 1939. With George Brent and Geraldine Fitzgerald in a Bette Davis triumph

4. ANGELS WASH THEIR FACES, 1939. With Ann Sheridan.

5. BROTHER RAT AND A BABY, '40. Met and (real-life) married Jane Wyman.

6. THE LIFE OF KNUTE ROCK-NE, 1940. This did it for him.

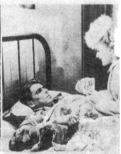

7. SANTA FE TRAIL, 1940. Gen- ￼ ...ter here resembled Reagan.

8. THE BAD MAN, 1941. Cowboy Ronald, Laraine Day in an MGM Western.

9. MILLION DOLLAR BABY, 1941. It was a $10 role. With Priscilla Lane here

After he starred in *Submarine D-1*, he started to receive fan mail from impressed fans. The next movie he made, his fourth movie, was *Hollywood Hotel*—his first "A" movie with Dick Powell. All his movies that followed were with famous co-stars, as well as filed on high budgets for successful results.

From there he went on to the film *Cowboy from Brooklyn* with Dick Powell and Pat O'Brien. This was the first time Ronald and Ann Sheridan co-starred together.[11111111]

Ron as George Gipp

---

[11] Hubler.

The Role I Liked Best . . .
BY RONALD REAGAN

[12]Ronald's first big money maker was *Brother Rat*, a comedy about Virginia Military Institute. Eddie Albert and Wayne Morris co-starred with him in *Brother Rat*, along with Jane Wyman. Following after was one of his best and favorite movies (*Knute Rochne: All American*), where he played the part of George Gipp, who they called "The Gipper."

He actually talked Warner Brothers into giving him the part of George Gipp. As you may remember, Ronald loved football and played it for years while attending high school and college. *Knute Rochne* was played by Pat O'Brien while telling the story and history of Notre Dame football team. George Gipp played

---

12 Hubler.

an important role in that history. He was greatly missed by all when his life ended and was used to inspire the whole team in successful outcomes. Knute Rochne would say, "Play one for the Gipper." Ronald received excellent reviews from the critics, as well as a lot more fan mail from the public.

Coming up right after *Knute Rochne* was his film, *The Sante Fe Trail*, with Earl Flynn and Olivia de Havilland. He was grateful for being selected to play the part of Lieutenant Custer which won him additional audience recognition.[13]

Scenes from "Sante Fe Trail"

---

[13] Hubler.

Ron was next loaned out from Warner Brothers to MGM for the film *The Badman*. He played the role of a near-bankrupt rancher with Lionel Barrymore and Lorraine Day. He returned to Warner Brothers to star in *Million Dollar Baby* with Priscilla Lane. He played a concert pianist. He did several pictures with the Dead End Kids, which were not his favorite experiences.[14]

The very next best picture came while starring with Bette Davis in *Dark Victory*, which included Humphrey Bogart. This film is still shown on the American Movie Classics (AMC) television channel.[15]

---

[14] Hubler.
[15] Hubler.

10. INTERNATIONAL SQUAD-
RON, 1941. He was now heading up.

11. NINE LIVES ARE NOT
ENOUGH, 1941. This was a snap.

12. KINGS ROW, 1941. Ann Sheridan,
here. His was the important role of *Drake*.

13. JUKE GIRL, 1942. Also
with Annie and but good.

14. DESPERATE JOURNEY, 1942. Errol Flynn,
Arthur Kennedy—Reagan's last before the war.

15. THIS IS THE ARMY, 1943.
The Army loaned him to Warners'.

16. STALLION ROAD, 1947. His first after the
war and together with Alexis Smith and Zachary Scott.

UNTO NIGHT, 1947. The imported Viveca
the honors in this with our Mr. Reagan.

Movie scenes from 1937-1947

His role about the Battle of Britain, titled *International Squadron*, in 1941, helped him into his favorite film, *Kings Row*.[16] According to Ronald, *Kings Row* in 1941 was the finest picture he ever made. In *Kings Row* he co-starred with Ann Sheridan and Robert Cummings. I was truly impressed with Ron in this film. The most outstanding scene in this film came when he woke up after an operation in which his character had lost both of his legs. He rehearsed this scene many times before he did it and called out to his co-star, Ann Sheridan, "Where's the rest of me?" His legs were amputated by a surgeon that did not want him around his daughter.[17]

Movie house photos from "Kings Row"

---

[16] Hubler.
[17] Hubler.

He did star in two other films, called *Nine Lives are Not Enough*, where he played the role of a gifted photographer, and *Murder in the Air* for Warner Brothers, where he was a sailor aboard the ship *Narcissus*.[18]

---

[18] Hubler.

Movie house photos of "Nine Lives Are Not Enough"

Movie house photos of "Murder in the Air"

Ronald co-starred with Ann Sheridan in *Juke Girl* in 1942, a movie about a migrant farmer. He and she looked forward to starring in the film together. He then filmed *Desperate Journey* with Earl Flynn.[19]

"Juke Girl"

His last picture for Warner Brothers before he went into the Army was *This is the Army*. The Army allowed him time away from service to film this one in 1943. It was a musical comedy and Warner Brothers gave all the profits to the Army Relief Fund.

One of the most important films of his career was next in 1947. It was called *Stallion Road* with Alexis Smith. This was the film that introduced him to "the most beautiful horse in the world," Tar Baby. She was a jumper, and he ended up buying this horse and making her one of his most prized possessions. It led to the purchase of his eight-acre ranch in

---

[19] Hubler.

Northridge while married to Jane Wyman. When married to Nancy Davis, he purchased a 300-acre ranch in Malibu Hills.

Here's my Tar Baby and *her* baby. The foal belongs to my wife, Jane Wyman, who has nicknamed it Piccia, meaning "little one."

My New Pal

by Ronald Reagan

★ Acting is my business, horse riding is my hobby. Sometimes I'm lucky enough to combine the two, and while making *Stallion Road*, I really hit the jackpot. Because then I met Tar Baby, and I'm proud to say we now belong to each other. We've been riding together for about a year, jumping fences and racing over the California hills. We were both glad to show off for *Screen Guide's* photographer.

Ronald Reagan Introduces Us To Tar Baby, The Mare He Describes As "the Most Beautiful Horse In the World." Could He Be Slightly Prejudiced?

Ron and Tar Baby

His second picture in 1947 was the very impressive *Night Unto Night*, with Viveca Linfors. In the first chapter of the book, I told everyone this is the film that started me toward being a dedicated fan of Ronald Reagan. I received that movie house scenes from one of the ushers who worked at the Perry Theater.

"Night Unto Night"

7   Arriving for John's dinner party, Ann meets Dr. Poole. Uninvited Lisa later overhears him describe to Ann John's illness, "which often strikes brilliant men."

10   When hurricane extinguishes lights, Ann and John go to attic for lamps. reveals she is aware of incurable disease; assures him of unchanging l

8 At dinner that evening, jealous, embittered ...a shocks the group by confes: her failure to arouse John's interest, cruely reveals nature of John's ailm

9 Enraged, Ann follows Lisa from the dining room after latter's untoward out burst, upbraids her sister for betraying John's secret to guests, slaps her face

A FLORIDA SETTING has been given "Night Unto Night" co-starring Ronald Reagan and Viveca Lindfors coming to the Stanley Friday. The film is based on a novel by Philip Wylie.

WARNER BROS. Present RONALD REAGAN · VIVECA LINDFORS in "NIGHT UNTO NIGHT"

The advertisement for the film said, "Whatever it is, there is nothing you can't tell the woman you love." What the ad is referring to is the actor's fact that he had to inform his love interest that he had an incurable disease called epilepsy.

Then came *The Voice of the Turtle*. With Ronald was Eleanor Parker. I really liked this movie; another film in 1947 that confirmed me a loyal fan of Ronald Reagan. Ronald plays a lonesome soldier. It ends up with Ronald changing Eleanor Parker's feelings of being fearful about a new love. Eve Arden co-starred with them.

The same year he starred in *That Hagan Girl* with Shirley Temple. It was the first grown-up role Shirley Temple played with Ronald. Even though she was a lot younger than him, he tried for romance for her first time.

Ron and Shirley Temple

In the winter of 1947–1948 he made another notable film, *John Loves Mary*, with Patricia Neal. This was one of my favorite films of Ron. Jack Carson played a friend of Ron's in the film. Edward Arnold played the father of Patricia Neal. John and Mary had a hard time working out their relationship, but it ended with good results and them getting married.

'JOHN LOVES MARY," a new Warner Bros. movie co-starring Patricia Neal, Ronald Reagan and Edward Arnold, above, with Jack Carson, is now showing at the Stanley Theater, Seventh St., Downtown. Arrangements are being completed with Manager Charlie Eagle and Warner Bros. for the next Sec! Hawkins' Child Welfare Group rally at the Stanley.

Ron loves Pat—or rather, "John Loves Mary"—a rollicking film version of the stage hit.

JOHN LOVES MARY (Warners) ♦♦♦

Get set for a fun evening! This story was adapted from the Broadway hit; and while the idea may be a bit aged, it's still worth the chuckles you'll give it.

When army man Ronald Reagan returns from the war, fiancée Pat Neal's waiting with open arms. She's all set to get married and settle down, but before she can do that, Ron has to figure out a way to get rid of the war bride he's brought back to U. S. Marrying an English lass was Ron's idea of doing a good deed for his buddy Jack Carson who loved the girl madly way back when. During a lapse of time, however, Jack returned to this country, fell in love and married someone else—without advising friend Ron about the switch. When Ron finds out the situation he's in a mess.

The problem is to keep Pat's senator father from discovering what's happened—and also to try to get the family to postpone the marriage. The threat of bigamy hangs heavy but there's a solution. Everything works out all right—although you might wonder how it possibly could!

In her first screen role, Pat Neal turns in a neat performance and assures herself of a steady movie career. (Her next will be "Fountainhead.") Edward Arnold, Ronald Reagan, Jack Carson and Wayne Morris help make this entertaining.

P. Neal and Ron in "John Loves Mary"

In the summer of 1948 Ronald's next picture turned out to be a box-office triumph. *The Girl from Jones Beach* co-starred Virginia Mayo, Eddie Bracken and Dona Drake. Virginia Mayo plays the part of a high school teacher. Ronald plays the part of an artist looking for an ideal model. And then he talked her into becoming his model and both ended up falling in love with each other. It was done and really is a comedy with great entertainment. The movie scene photo was personally autographed by Virginia Mayo. The scenes on the beach and of all of them swimming won Ronald the title of "Hollywood's Best-Built Male" at that time.

"The Girl from Jones Beach"

1. Impoverished promoter Chuck Donovan (Eddie Bracken) will collect $10,000 if he can sign artist Bob Randolph (Ronald eagan) and his famed Randolph Girl model to a television ontract. Bob refuses, for his creation is a composite of 12 girls.

2. Next morning, in a rowboat off Jones Beach, Chuck spots an in-the-flesh version of the Randolph Girl through field glasses. She disappears before Chuck reaches shore. He calls Bob. They haunt the beach until they find her—Ruth Wilson (Virginia Mayo).

3. Ruth is a teacher who wants to be admired for intellectual rather than physical attributes. Learning that she teaches an evening naturalization class, Bob contrives to get her to pose. When Ruth discovers his identity, she's in love—and doesn't care.

4. Ruth thinks she's loved for her brain—and now doesn't like the idea. Still not realizing just why Bob enrolled, she asks him to meet her at the beach, hoping to use the evening blindness to her beauty. Meantime Bob and Chuck plan the book and marry her.

5. When Chuck hears the meeting being arranged, he and his girl Connie Martin (Dona Drake) arrive with newspapermen and cameras. The resulting publicity causes Ruth's school board to dismiss her from her position. It also ends her romance with Bob.

Ruth takes her dismissal to court where, in a bathing suit, she's Exhibit A. Bob comes to her defense and the judge (Henry Travers) upholds her right to teach. After a surprise twist, Ruth and Bob reconcile as Chuck and Connie plan to make it a double wedding.

Just like kids, Ronnie, Virginia, Eddie and Dona join hands and make a wild dash into the water—last one in is a bugs, you know. The lively foursome were at Balboa making "The Girl From Jones Beach," for Warners.

Hollywood's
BEST-BUILT
MALES

In the new Warner comedy "The Girl from Jones Beach" Virginia Mayo gets plenty of opportunity to display her pulchritude and charms—but the Ronald Reagan torso is also in evidence, in line with the current Hollywood trend to undrape the muscular hero.

Virginia tries her skill at an old beach game and finds the big leap hard to make.

Next on Ronald Reagan's agenda was starring in *The Hasty Heart*. He traveled to England aboard the *S.S. Britannica* with Patricia Neal. Ron played the part of Yank in this film. Richard Todd played the Scotsman who loved his nurse (Patricia Neal). When Ronald finds himself in a hospital, the scene is very dramatic and very well done, like his *Kings Row* after-surgery scene. The *Press* newspaper claimed it was a sellout movie for charity with all the proceeds going for crippled children in Pittsburgh. Ronald was very pleased with that when I wrote him of the great amount given to the crippled children. Patricia Neal and Ronald returned home aboard the *Queen Mary*. Ronald truly enjoyed the ride home aboard the *Queen Mary* much more than his adventures aboard the *S.S. Britannica*.

Ronald Reagan and Pat Neal returned from England on the
Queen Mary after making *The Hasty Heart* for Warners. Pat's
currently making a hit in *The Fountainhead* and Ronald's in
Ring in the New. Friends still hope he and Jane will reconcile

THERE ARE MANY **TENSE MOMENTS** in the Warner Bros. film, "The Hasty Heart."
Above is a scene from the movie which will be given its world premiere by Press Old News-
boys at the Warner Theater Wednesday night, Dec. 14. Stars include Ronald Reagan,
Richard Todd and Patricia Neal.

Scenes from "The Hasty Heart"

All Proceeds for Crippled Kiddies—

'The Hasty Heart' Movie Premiere Complete Sellout by Old Newsboys

Bryant's Wildcats, Dingbat on Program

The Press Old Newsboys' movie premiere of Warner Bros., "The Hasty Heart" at the Warner Theater tonight is a complete sellout.

The annual movie premiere always is one of the big highlights of the drive Old Newsboys stage to raise funds for Pittsburgh district crippled children.

Doors at the theater will be open at 7:30 o'clock. The program will begin promptly at 8:30. Tickets are distributed by Old Newsboys. If they have any left over they will be sold at the box office.

Slim Bryant and his KDKA Wildcats will entertain from the stage. Donnie Dingbat, The Press weatherbird, also will be on hand to act as master of ceremonies for the show. It will mark the animated Donnie's first appearance at the Old Newsboys' premiere.

Great Warner Picture

"The Hasty Heart" movie is one of those pictures which comes along once in a decade to leap right out from among the better ones as a film not to be missed.

It has as its stars Ronald Reagan and Patricia Neal and the British actor Richard Todd who plays the role of a dour Scotsman.

It is a dramatic picture packed with both laughs and tears. It's the story of five men in a hospital, men from as many countries, who must keep a secret from one of their number, the Scot who has fallen in love

STARRING ROLES IN OLD NEWSBOYS' MOVIE premiere of the Warner Bros. film "The Hasty Heart" at Warner Theater tonight are played by Ronald Reagan and Richard Todd, top left to right, and Patricia Neal. All proceeds of show go to Children's Hospital.

with the nurse, played by Miss Neal.

Reagan As 'Yank'

Ronald Reagan plays the role of a light-hearted Yank who finds himself stranded in the hospital. He turns in what many regard as his greatest performance since his peak role in "Kings Row."

Todd, in playing the difficult role of the Scotsman, seems headed for an Academy Award.

Others in the strong supporting cast include Anthony Nichols, Howard Marion-Crawford, Ralph Michael, John Sherman and Orlando Martin.

The movie was filmed in England under the direction of Vincent Sherman.

LEADING ROLES IN PRESS OLD NEWSBOYS' MOVIE PREMIERE, "The Hasty Heart," are played by Ronald Reagan, Richard Todd and Patricia Neal, above, left to right. They are shown in one of the scenes from the picture. Old Newsboys' will present the film at the Warner Theater Wednesday night, Dec. 14.

Newsboys Plan Movie Premiere

(Continued from Page One)

finds himself stranded in the hospital. In this film he turns in what is said to be his greatest performance since his peak role in "Kings Row."

Highlight Every Year

The world premiere of a top flight film each year has been a highlight of the annual Press Old Newboys' drive to help Pittsburgh district crippled children. Other great films that have been premiered in the past include "The Adventures of Don Juan," starring Errol Flynn, last year; "My Wild Irish Rose," in which Dennis Morgan was starred; and "Spellbound," "Destination Toyko," and others.

The Old Newboys' campaign started 23 years ago. Since that time leading Pittsburghers annually take part in it, bent on giving aid to the boys and girls who require hospital treatment

---

HELP CRIPPLED CHILDREN

You may send your contribution for Children's Hospital direct to The Press. It will be credited to the Old Newsboy you designate. Make checks or money orders payable to "The Press — Children's Hospital Fund."

Name ....

Street ....

City ....

Credit to:.................
(Old Newsboys' Name Here)

Mail to:
Old Newsboys' Fund, Box 398, The Press, Pittsburgh 30, Pa.

---

took care of 47 per cent of the hospital's free work last year.

The Old Newboys raise their fund in many ways. One of these is through the annual movie premiere. Another is by direct solicitation of their friends. Other events designed to raise money are staged by various Old Newsboys.

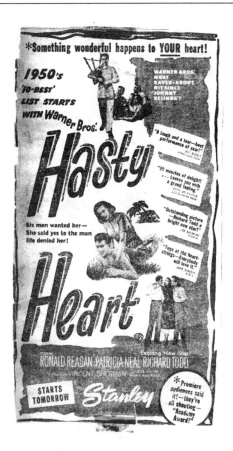

It was right after Ronald returned home that he played the charity baseball game for the benefit of City of Hope Hospital. He fell off first base with a multiple fracture of his right thigh. Ron spent months in traction, with a year of physical therapy before he regained 85-percent capacity to bend his knee.

The first movie after he shattered his knee and thigh was another one from Warner Brothers, called *Storm Warning*, co-starring Ginger Rogers, Doris Day and Steve Cochran. It was the history of the Ku Klux Klan, a story of how the Klan operated and the results of all their actions.

Movie house photos of "Storm Warning"

Now with an agreement made with Universal Studios, his next venture was to star in the movie *Louisa*, co-starring Piper Laurie, who played his daughter, and Spring Byington, who played the role of "Louisa" in the film. Ruth Hussey played Ronald's wife. It was a successful comedy.

Hal Norton (Ron Reagan) and wife, Meg (Ruth Hussey), hope his mother Louisa (Spring Byington) will stop interfering and find an "outside interest."

Mother's new interest turns out to be a beau, Henry Hammond (Edmund Gwenn). Now her family is furious with her.

Louisa gets involved in a love triangle when Hal's boss, Abel Burnside (Charles Coburn), gets romantic about her, too.

Abel sweeps Louisa off her feet. Looks like poor Henry doesn't stand a chance unless Arthur Murray comes to the rescue.

Faint heart ne'er won fair lady, so the two elderly bucks risk apoplexy, quarrel over Louisa. Abel wins the fight, but it's Henry who rates her sympathy.

Son Hal finally is convinced that Mother has found her outside interest. He and Meg see Louisa safely married to Henry.

MOTHER IS A PROBLEM

Mother has her day—and it's a romantic one—in Universal-International's hilarious film frolic, "Louisa"

Meg and Hal live happily ever after. Even problems of their teen-age daughter are easier to handle than loves of Louisa.

Movie magazine photos of "Louisa"

It was a big night in Hollywood when "Louisa" was previewed—invitations included everyone's entire family. Ronnie Reagan, the star, took his mother and leading lady, pert Piper Laurie

Ronald and Moms Nelle

His next starring role was in *The Last Outpost*. Ronald played a confederate Cavalry Captain. Ronda Fleming co-starred with him. The horse he used in the film was his very own horse, Tar Baby. It certainly was not the first film in which Tar Baby was featured, but is was one of her best ones. It was a big-money return. I know you have seen Ronald with Tar Baby several times in this book.

Movie house photos of "The Last Outpost"

Next was another Warner Brothers film, *Working Her Way Through College*, with Virginia Mayo and Gene Nelson. It was a very good story of how Virginia Mayo managed her way through her college years. The Technicolor scenes were very well done.

Universal came to Ronald and offered him his next film, *Bedtime for Bonzo*, co-starring Diana Lynn and Walter Slezak. It was a story of a chimpanzee being raised in a home environment with the results that Bonzo's ability to learn was a lot better than in an animal environment.

Then came *Hong King*, co-starring Ronda Fleming. It was a story about Chinese Reds and included a four-year-old Chinese child actor, Danny Chong.

Next on his list was a baseball biography about Grover Cleveland Alexander. Doris Day was his co-star, playing the part of Grover Cleveland Alexander's wife. It told the story about Alexander's physical and mental problems because of his ailment, epilepsy. The film included a dozen big-league players.

Ronald next starred in a film called *Tropic Zone*, about a banana plantation and all the problems and solutions the story brought out.

The following movie with Universal was *Law and Order*, co-starring Dorothy Malone and Preston Foster. It was one of Ronald's western favorites.

Last but not least of Ronald's films was *Prisoner of War* about soldiers that were imprisoned in the Korean War. It was his last film before being hired by General Electric for GE Theater.

He not only MC'd all of the television films, but he also starred in some of them. It later developed into Ronald doing lecturing tours for GE employees all over the United States.

Ronald made a total of 50 films in movies and television before he retired and entered the world of politics.

At Warner Bros. Ronald Reagan and Johnny "Scat" Davis help brother John Payne get in shape with a between-scenes workout, for his role in pic, *Kid Nightingale*.

32 MOVIES

Ron with John Davis and John Payne

One of the items I want to show you is Ronald at Warner Brothers helping John Payne get in shape with a between-scenes workout—another example of Ronald's humanitarian efforts to all he was around and any job he was doing. John Payne went on to star in his own film, *Kid Nightingale*, which was all about athletics.

The second item in the opinion and experience of Virginia Mayo, Ronald's co-star in *The Girl from Jones Beach*, was when Virginia Mayo signed a contract with Warner Brothers. Her first picture assignment of importance to her was the lead in *The Girl from Jones Beach* opposite Ronald Reagan. She was aware of and had heard a great deal of praise for Ronnie, but in her opinion, no one has ever quite told the full story of his sweetness and generosity. Ronnie restored her self-confidence by pointing out all her abilities and that she was an attractive, talented actress. He also convinced her of her good personality that helped her continue to be a successful actress with little or no self-doubt whatsoever.

Another good example of Ronnie's ability to help and assist anyone working with him is that from all of this he went on to be a political humanitarian.

FIVE

Heaven's Gift to the State of California

EFFECTIVE LEADERSHIP: From all his political experience, between being President of the SAG and then working for the GE Theater and going on all the lecturing tours across the United States, Ronald Reagan became born again. After being offered the opportunity to run for Governor on January 2, 1967, Ronald became the Governor of California.

He was still the warmest, most amiable, kindest person you would ever meet, plus the fact that he brought into his governorship his Bible study and Christian beliefs for all his goals. He was a man who liked order and security for all.

Before becoming Governor, he campaigned in 1964 for Barry Goldwater, with good results. Ronald knew his movie career ended for a good reason. I believe his movie-star life ended because God sent and meant him to help and save the American people in a lot of ways.

Even though the people were very upset by the fact that his wife, Nancy, refused to live in the Governor's mansion, I know she must have had important reasons not to live there with her family. She felt it was much better for them all to live in Sacramento, California.

Ronald started on his way to exercise his Christian goal as "American Rescuer." Ronald's welfare bill ended up saving the taxpayers two billion dollars in California. Here, in the reports of his efforts and their results, are the "Know the Facts" from *In the Spirit of the 70s*, titled, "Withholding and the Fair Share Tax Reform Package." Governor Reagan was always philosophically opposed to withholding. He faced a choice between a ten percent increase in the income tax or obtaining the same amount of revenue with no increase in the present rates. He could not in good conscience advocate the increase.

[20]Therefore, he proposed withholding as the means of making possible property tax reductions and renter relief as set forth in the "Fair Share Tax Reform Package" before the legislature. The results of this entire package:

(1) The Governor will continue to oppose any withholding propositions designed to produce money for spending programs rather than tax relief.

(2) Because the taxpayer is less aware of his tax burden when it is paid through a payroll deduction plan, Governor Reagan asked for a law requiring a two-thirds majority vote before the Legislature can enact any future tax increases.

(3) In recent years, the amount of state revenues from the income tax increased thirty percent. This accentuated the cash flow problem and forced the state to increase its borrowing during the lean months. There would be considerable savings to the taxpayers in reduced interest charges as a result of withholding.

---

[20] Levy, Peter, *Encyclopedia of Reagan-Bush Years,* (Westport, CT: Greenwood Press, 1996).

(4) There was a windfall in the transition year when withholding went into effect. One-hundred percent of this one-time windfall was returned to the taxpayers. In April 1971, each citizen deducted about thirty-five percent of his tax just as he deducted ten percent this past April. As nearly as can be figured now, the rebate was more than $400 million.

The State adopted these other major tax relief programs during the Reagan Administration:

(1) Provided a $70.00 refund to homeowners to offset high property taxes.

(2) Adopted a permanent $750.00 per dwelling property tax exemption, beginning in 1970.

(3) Authorized relief for renters by permitting increased standard-form income tax reduction.

(4) Adopted a special program of property tax relief for low-income senior citizens and reduced rates of the lowest-income tax bracket.

(5) Reduced the business inventory tax by 30 percent, a bipartisan program to save warehouse and storage jobs that California had been losing to nearby states which do not tax inventories. Business—not personal income—taxpayers financed this, through accelerated corporate tax collections.

It added up to $633 million in direct tax relief under Reagan's Administration. How did Ronald Reagan do all this? Here is how it was done. Governor Reagan faced up to the chaotic financial situations with integrity and determination. With its credit and national economic image at stake, California had to put its financial affairs in order, balance the budget as the Constitution required, reduce government's growth and start living with its income. To accomplish this, Governor Reagan:

(1) Ordered budget cuts for most departments, continuing economy measures that saved $130 million.

(2) Recruited, without state cost, a task force of business specialists to survey state methods and recommend economics. The result—$187 million saved in the first 33 months.

(3) Obtained legislative approval of the long-overdue tax increase necessary to balance the budget.

(4) Vetoed more than $325 million in legislative spending proposals that would have required tax increases. The State's accounting system lists such tax relief measures as the $70.00 per homeowner refund as expenditures, which raised state budget total. In reality, though, these terms "reduced" the individual's taxes.

All of this resulted in this quote from the *Oakland Tribune*: "Governor Ronald Reagan's persistent economy efforts are turning the tide against bureaucracy in California's state government."

FROM "IN THE SPIRIT OF THE 70s," KNOW THESE FACTS

Unemployment Facts—Did you know:

❑ Unemployment during the first 42 months of the Reagan Administration averaged 4.7 percent.

❑ Unemployment during the previous administration (1959–1967) averaged 5.8 percent. During 1968–1969, unemployment was down to 4.4 percent, the lowest monthly average for California in more than a decade. This happened under the Reagan Administration.

❏ Months in which California unemployment rates were five percent or higher: Under the Brown Unruh Administration (1959–1967) 78 of 96 months, or 81.2 percent; the Reagan Administration (1967–1970) 11 of 43 months, or 25.5 percent.

❏ Months in which California unemployment rate was 5.9 percent or higher: Under previous administration (1960–1966) 50 out of 84 months, or 59 percent (last seven years); the Reagan Administration (1967–1970) three of 43 months, or seven percent.

❏ Months when California unemployment rate was 6.2 percent or higher: Under the Brown Unruh Administration (1959–1967) 21 of last 72 months, or 29.1 percent; the Reagan Administration (1967–1970) three of 43 months, or 2.3 percent.

PEOPLE AND PAYCHECKS

❏ California civilian employment soared past the eight million mark in 1969. Wages were up. Personal income went up nine percent per year.

❏ Numerous Californians, many of them racial minority citizens, have not shared that prosperity.

❏ Under the Reagan Administration, state-operated manpower projects are being reorganized into his effective program to help the hard-core jobless earn a fair share. Other measures were enacted to:

(1) Encourage small business to train and hire long-term unemployed by allowing a state tax deduction of part of the cost.

(2) Ban discrimination in apprentice programs.

(3) Provide state seed money to encourage bank investment in the Cal-Job program at no State cost.

By executive action, Ronald Reagan:

(1) Named more minority citizens to policy-making positions than any other California Governor.

(2) Appointed the first Negro State Department Head.

(3) Benefited from the able services of minority citizens in key positions on his personal staff.

Reagan also supported programs to improve the quality of metropolitan-area life. The following are examples:

(1) The California Factory-Built Housing Law that established the first uniform state code prefabricated structure. The result, reduced costs through mass production.

(2) A major program to encourage new, totally planned communities with built-in open spaces.

(3) Project Sandlot for state local park and playground development on surplus state land.

(4) Relocation assistance and realistic compensation for people forced to move by freeway construction.

All of this resulted in the Work Incentive (WIN) Program, aimed at finding jobs for employable persons receiving AFDC welfare funds. In its first year, 4,500 welfare recipients became permanently employed. This shift, from welfare rolls to payrolls, saved $2,600.00 per year per family. Governor Reagan revamped California's costly welfare programs. The goals:

(1) Reduce welfare costs by eliminating fraud and by streamlining the administration system.

(2) Encourage and emphasize efforts to phase people out of welfare programs and into productive employment.

(3) Provide for long-term needs of the aged, blind and other permanently disabled, with a minimum of red tape and a maximum of concern for the individual's dignity.

Putting all California's financial affairs in order:

(1) Ordered budget costs for most departments and continuing economy measures that saved an initial $130 million.

(2) Recruited, without state cost, a task force of business specialists to survey state methods and recommend economies. The result, $187 million saved in the first 33 months.

(3) Obtained legislative approval of the long-overdue tax increase necessary to balance the budget.

(4) Received legislative approval of reorganization plans to make government more efficient and provide better service. One 1969 program eliminated 29 boards and commissions.

(5) Vetoed more than $325 million in legislative spending proposals that would have required tax increases.

All of these items reduced the individual taxes. As governor, Ronald raised tuition rates that gave him a hard time.

After that, he related to the youth very well. The 1969 Student Strike in California inspired Ronald to send in the Highway Patrol and the National Guard at Berkeley. He restored peace at Berkeley College and became their hero. The following November, he went to cut back government taxes.

EDUCATION POLICIES

(1) State spending for higher education increased 54 percent under Governor Reagan. Other state functions averaged an 18-percent increase.

(2) The budget provided $12.9 million for student scholarships and loans; 57.5 percent above the previous year.

State Colleges:

(1) State General Fund support for the University of California was $329.8 million, up nearly $39 million above the previous year. Dollar increase was 13.3 percent, compared to estimated 5-6 percent enrollment increase.

(2) State College received $288 million, a boost of more that $46 million over the previous year. This was 24 percent more money for one percent more students.

Crit Before events and page *what Ronald did for schools in Calif. with* *(# 81)*

"Our nation is founded on
a concern for the individual
and his right to fulfillment,
and this should be the
preoccupation of our schools
and colleges."

Ronald Reagan

To show you the further accomplishment by Ronald in school support from *In the Spirit of the 70s*—"Know the Facts": Governor Reagan campaigned for and worked to attain the state's total percentage of public school costs reached to 50-percent level in the mid-1950s.

Over four budget years, the Reagan Administration provided $533.2 million of increased aid to schools, about $176.2 million more than the total increase in school aid during the final four budget years of former Governor Brown's administration.

From Governor Reagan's Effective Leadership titled "Crisis on Campus," you can see the efforts and the results put forth by Ronald Reagan.

Governor Reagan made clear his determined stand against those seeking to disrupt and destroy our university and college campuses by violence. "The learning process" he declares, "cannot function in an atmosphere of terrorism or intimidation." Then came "Action from the Capital." The 1969 legislature acted on Governor Reagan's recommendations for legal tools to combat campus violence. Bills signed into law included these:

(1) Required discipline of students, faculty or employees convicted of campus crimes.

(2) Suspended state financial support for convicted students.

(3) Required distribution of specific rules of conduct on all campuses.

(4) Made it illegal for anyone ejected from a campus for a disturbance to return within 72 hours. This action was aimed at repeat offenders.

(5) Clarified the placing of a bomb that results in a death as first-degree murder.

(6) Provided state reimbursement to local police for part of the extra costs in furnishing requested emergency assistance.

(7) Tightened loopholes in statutes against unlawful assembly.

(8) Made it a crime to coerce by threats officials or teachers at any educational institution.

(9) Extended California's ban on paramilitary groups to campus organizations which engaged in violence.

(10) Outlawed possession of loaded firearms in schools and other public places.

(11) Permitted counties to offer rewards for the arrest and conviction of persons committing criminal acts against public employees.

This is how Ronald Reagan added to his becoming a hero for all schools. A quote from Arthur Ribbel, titled "Sharper, Tougher": "California's governor, Ronald Reagan, has become more seasoned, sharper, tougher and wiser after undergoing the tribulation of one of the most difficult government jobs."

No matter how you slice it, under the Reagan Administration, California spent more on higher education, the university and state college system, than at any other time in its history.

Elementary Schools:

(1) Introduced new elementary school textbooks that put more stress on phonics in the teaching of reading. Average reading scores dramatically turned upward.

(2) Created a Commission on Educational Reform to make an independent review of the entire system of

elementary and secondary schools and recommend improvements.*

A SAFER STATE—FROM "IN THE SPIRIT OF THE 70s"

Governor Reagan mobilized the full force of state government in the battle against crime, violence and obscenity in California. These included two anti-pornography laws, the first of such success in eight years. The new measures established a definition for pornography and made it a crime to knowingly distribute such harmful material to minors under 18 years old.

Other crime measures enacted with Reagan's support:

(1) Proclaimed the authority of local governments to regulate topless and bottomless entertainment.

(2) Permitted courts to grant immunity to witnesses willing to testify on the activities of crime organizations such as the Mafia.

(3) Permitted authorities, under certain circumstances, to protect the anonymity of police informers—an essential step to prevent possible gangland retribution.

(4) Increased penalty from "Five years to Life" to "15 years to Life" for rape, robbery and burglary if the victim suffered bodily injury.

(5) Made it illegal for unauthorized persons to carry loaded firearms into schools or other public places.

(6) Outlawed the possession of machine guns or machine-gun parts.

---

* Reference to Footnote 20 concluded at this point.

The 1969 Legislature, with its new Republican majorities, provided a milestone in Governor Reagan's efforts to enact tougher, more realistic laws to fight crime in California. With Reagan's support, the lawmakers enacted the most significant anti-crime legislation in more than a decade. Under Governor Reagan, California also took these major steps to fight crime:

(1) Established the California Council on Criminal Justice to develop a master plan to improve crime prevention, detection and control.

(2) Created the California Crime Technological Research Foundation to help local enforcement with modern scientific equipment and techniques.

(3) Added law enforcement experience to parole and probation policies by putting former FBI and police experts on the Adult Authority.

(4) Revamped communications and liaisons between state and local officials to provide large, effective forces for riots, natural disasters or other major disorders.

(5) Established the nation's first computer-to-computer crime information lookup.

Crime Prevention:

Under Governor Reagan, prevention was a necessary part of the battle against crime. California, under Reagan's leadership:

(1) Earmarked $200,000 to finance the state's first juvenile delinquency prevention programs.

(2) Established a program of 72-hour pre-release leaves so prisoners could prepare for their return to society by interviewing for jobs and securing such necessities as driver's license, housing and union clearance.

(3) Broadened the work furlough program permitting inmates, during the final months of their terms, to learn to earn a nest egg for their start on a new life.

A HEALTHIER STATE

Chaos created by the last enactment of the Medi-Cal program confronted Governor Reagan when he took office. Claim payments lagged six months behind schedule. Controls on spending and functions were insufficient. Advance precautions against fraud and misuse were lacking. The program was underfunded by some $86 million. The new Reagan Administration went into action. The results:

(1) Processing time for 81 percent of all Medi-Cal claims was cut to 30 working days.

(2) A computerized billing system rejected $1.4 million per month in duplicate claims that otherwise would have been paid.

(3) The claim filing period was shortened from six months to 60 days.

(4) A surveillance bureau was organized to detect abuses by those who provided services. With support from the Medi-Cal profession, strict laws were enacted in 1969 to crack down on Medi-Cal abuses and fraud.

(5) A pilot prepaid health-insurance contract was established in a four-county area, providing high-quality medical care to eligible residents at less than the amount budgeted. In fact, preliminary estimates indicated that 200,000 or more would be returned to the state.

(6) Extensive management reorganization put Medi-Cal in the black for 1967–1968. A tentative report indicated

1968–1969 expenditures also were well within the budget.

Improved Expansion: The Reagan Administration also improved the operation and expanded the scope of other programs designed to make this a healthier state. Since 1967, California has:

(1) Doubled state-administered immunization programs for measles and other children's diseases. One result was that measles cases dropped from a range of 22,000–68,000 per year to 1,500 cases in 1968.

(2) Increased by more than 10,000 annually the number of persons successfully rehabilitated in state programs for the physically and mentally disabled, including former alcoholics and drug addicts.

(3) Made the alcoholic rehabilitation program permanent.

(4) Established, in cooperation with federal and local authorities, health service clinics for migratory farm workers and other families.

(5) Enacted legislation implementing Proposition 5 to permit the state to insure up to $150 million in privately-financed hospital construction and renovation loans.

WAR ON NARCOTICS

Drug abuse is probably the most critical social problem of our time. It is nearing epidemic proportions among your people. Here is what is being done:

(1) Legislation under Ronald Reagan's procedures for a family to obtain involuntary detention and treatment of a juvenile user without causing his arrest.

(2) Working with the PTA, medial and police officer associations, Governor Reagan has encouraged senior and junior high schools to form drug-abuse councils. Purpose: Develop local educational programs to combat student drug usage.

(3) The administration established the Interagency Drug Abuse Council, representatives of involved state agencies, medical professions, law enforcement, local government, church and civic groups, to coordinate an assault at all levels.

(4) Fostered a $2 million education program without cost to the state to dramatize drug danger warnings to youngsters by television, radio, newspaper and pamphlets. Advertising and media executives and television personalities donated their services.

TOUGHER NEW LAWS

Governor Reagan's Administration sponsored and supported tougher laws to crack down on those who profit off the human tragedy of drug addiction. Examples:

(1) Increased penalties for dangerous drug pushers.

(2) School principals permitted to expel or suspend students caught selling narcotics or dangerous drugs on school grounds.

(3) Prohibits juveniles under 18 years old from entering Mexico without parents' written consent. From Cliff Smith, *LA Herald-Examiner*—"Governor Reagan has turned out to be one of the hardest-working governors we have had."

A CLEANER, GREENER STATE—THE WAR AGAINST SMOG

Under Governor Reagan's leadership, California:

(1) Established the Air Resources Board, with new powers to enforce the state's air pollution regulations, already the nation's strongest. The board made them still tougher.

(2) Recruited some of the world's foremost scientists to help guide California's efforts to eliminate smog. Reagan appointees include Nobel Prize Winner, Dr. Willard Libby (UCLA), and A.J. Haagen-Smith (Cal Tech)—the scientists who discovered smog origins in the Los Angeles Basin.

(3) Enacted the nation's first program to control air pollution from jet aircraft.

(4) Secured a waiver permitting California to enforce its own tough smog controls, rather than the weaker federal standards.

(5) Began experiments to determine if smogless, steam-powered vehicles might be a satisfactory substitute for internal combustion engines.

FOR CLEANER WATER

The Reagan Administration drafted and the 1969 Legislature passed the comprehensive California Water Quality Act—the first revision of the state's water laws in 20 years. During the Reagan Administration, the state took three steps:

(1) Suspended offshore oil exploration on state property in the Santa Barbara Channel and reiterated Reagan's proposal that the state have authority to inspect federal offshore drilling.

(2) Doubled the penalties imposed by the Fish and Game Code for Pollution.

(3) Suspended oil leasing in San Pablo Bay. The bay was saved.

In 1969, broader powers to protect the San Francisco Bay from unnecessary filling and dredging. Reagan represented a tough bill which:

(1) Modified scores of state projects to protect scenic and natural resources.

(2) Created the Environmental Quality Study Council to recommend improvement of our natural environment.

(3) Established a bi-state agency to develop a plan of environmental protection for the Lake Tahoe Basin.

HELP FOR THE HELPLESS

Governor Reagan strongly supports this humanitarian effort to provide prompt diagnostics and treatment for the mentally ill close to their families and homes. Examples of higher-level help totally supported by Reagan for California's mentally ill:

(1) The last pre-Reagan budget provided $15 million in state aid for community mental health programs. The 1969–1970 Reagan budget provided $53.4 million, an increase of more than 300 percent in three years.

(2) In 1967, total state funding for the Department of Mental Hygiene was $213.6 million for 1969–1970. It is now $265 million.

(3) During the final year of the previous administration, there were 13,449 employees for 26,567 mental patients or, roughly, one employee for every two patients. In 1969, there were 10,483 authorized positions in hospitals for mentally ill to serve a patient population of only 16,927. The ratio equals one employee for 1.6 patients.

(4) The budget authorized 785 new positions (mostly nursing personnel) to further increase the quality of patient care.

(5) The Reagan Administration adopted higher staffing standards, recommended by the California Hospital Standards Commission, and reached 94 percent of these higher standards in hospitals for the mentally ill. Even the previous lower standards were not achieved by the prior administration.

Help for the mentally retarded came in when Governor Reagan took office in 1967. California hospitals for the mentally retarded were overcrowded and understaffed. Many of the mentally retarded (a separate category of the mental health program) were housed in antiquated facilities. The task of correcting this long-developing situation was enormous. Yet, within three years, the Reagan Administration had achieved significant improvements.

STANDARDS, FUNDS INCREASED

(1) Between 1967 and 1969, the number of authorized treatment positions (nursing personnel, etc.) increased by 933, raising care standards to a new high.

(2) The 1966–1967 budget for the mentally-retarded hospital system was $50.8 million. In 1968, it was $62.5 million.

(3) Nine local diagnostic and counseling centers for the mentally retarded opened in San Diego, Los Angeles, San Francisco, San Jose, Fresno, Sacramento, Redding, Orange County, and one served the San Luis Obispo, Santa Barbara, and Ventura county areas.

(4) State appropriations for community mental retardation clinics were doubled.

(5) A new four-story research center at the Neuro-Psychiatric Institute in Los Angeles served 100 patients a month.

(6) The previous administration provided an average of $9.68 per day per patient to care for the mentally retarded. The 1969–1970 budget, reflecting a higher level of care, averaged $16.24.

Another tremendous example of Ronald Reagan's humanitarianism.

PROTECTING THE CONSUMER

Under Governor Reagan's leadership, California led the nation with effective state programs to protect the consumer against fraud, misrepresentation, false advertising, and unfair business practices.

LAWS STRENGTHENED

The 1969 Legislature, under new Republican leadership, passed and Governor Reagan signed new laws that:

(1) Tightened public protection in home improvement contracts and buying and canceling insurance.

(2) Strengthened laws governing labels on prescriptions and purity in pet foods.

(3) Protected the consumer against being unfairly charged for goods or services billed to a stolen, lost or unsolicited and unused credit card.

(4) Implemented new federal laws on credit installment sales, fair packaging and labeling.

(5) Protected the public against unethical land promoters selling rural or subdivision property located in remote areas.

(6) Prohibited real estate agents from forcing buyers to purchase insurance through a particular insurer, agent, broker or solicitor.

(7) Required insurance companies to maintain minimum financial reserves to protect California policyholders.

(8) Strengthened policyholders' rights against auto insurance cancellation.

Administrative action to protect the privacy of individuals. Governor Reagan ordered the Department of Motor Vehicles to stop selling lists of driver's license holders for commercial purposes. Bipartisan approval was signaled by Assemblyman LeRoy F. Greens, Sacramento Democrat, who stated, "We all owe a vote of thanks to Governor Reagan."

Some examples:

(1) A soldering solution containing cyanide was removed from sale in California until the manufacturers developed elaborate precautionary labeling.

(2) A large quantity of toys was quarantined when state investigators found a potential eye irritant present without proper warning. Statement from columnist Nick Thimmesch, *Running Well.*

Get-tough legislation on student unrest and pornography was passed. Under Reagan's leadership, strong conservation and consumer protection bills were enacted. Even Reagan's enemies privately admitted that the state government was running well.

PEOPLE AND PAYCHECKS

California civilian employment soared past the eight-million mark in 1969. Wages were up nine percent in a year. But numerous Californians—many of them racial minority citizens—had not fully shared this prosperity. Under the Reagan Administration, state-operated manpower projects were reorganized into an effective program to help the hard-core jobless earn a fair share.

NEW JOBS GENERATED

Other measures were enacted to:

(1) Encourage small businesses to train and hire long-term unemployed by allowing a state tax deduction of part of the cost.

(2) Ban discrimination in apprentice programs.

(3) Provide state seed money to encourage bank investment in the Cal-Job program at no state cost.

(4) Named more minority citizens to policy-making positions than any other California governor.

(5) Appointed the first Negro state department head.

(6) Benefited from the able services of minority citizens in key positions on his personal staff.

Reagan also supported programs to improve the quality of metropolitan-area life. Some examples:

(1) The California Factory-Built Housing Law established the first uniform state code for prefabricated structures. The result was reduced costs through mass production.

(2) A major program encouraged new, totally planned communities with built-in open spaces.

(3) Project Sandlot, for state local park and playground development on surplus state land.

(4) Relocation assistance and realistic compensation for people forced to move by freeway construction.

WELFARE ROLLS TO PAYROLLS

The Work Incentive (WIN) Program was aimed at finding jobs for employable persons receiving AFDC welfare funds. In the first year, 4,500 welfare recipients became permanently employed. This shift, from welfare rolls to payrolls, saved $2,600 per year per family.

Governor Reagan

A HAND UP—NOT A HANDOUT

(1) Provided for long-term needs of the aged, blind and other permanently disabled, with a minimum of red tape and a maximum of concern for the individual's needs.

(2) Enacted a Reagan Administration bill designed to insure that funds intended to help needy children were not diverted for use by an unrelated male living with a welfare family. Reorganized the Department of Social Welfare with a greater emphasis on job and rehabilitation services.

(3) Implemented a statewide protective services program for all children subject to neglect or abuse.

(4) Launched a pilot project to provide financial help to low-income families qualified but financially unable to adopt hard-to-place children.

(5) A central registry was established of available adoptive homes, to extend placement opportunities to counties lacking adoption services.

Ron and Nancy in Kansas City

SAFE, SCENIC, SENSIBLE

Moving Californians is a complex challenge. Through action, the Reagan Administration demonstrated a recognition that the problem had to be attacked on several fronts. The Reagan Administration worked for a transportation system that was safe, preserved the state's scenic beauty, and achieved a planned, sensible balance of all methods of moving people and material.

SAFETY RECORD

(1) California's traffic fatality rate (based on vehicle miles of travel) reached 20 percent below the US average.

(2) Even the number of California traffic deaths dropped between 1967 and 1968 (from 4,883 to 4,853) while the national toll increased five percent.

(3) Pedestrian deaths (often involving children) dropped from 340 in 1966 to 295 in 1967 and further declined to 286 in 1968.

(4) California's freeway fatalities were 115 percent below the US rate for all roadways.

(5) The 1969 Legislature passed Reagan's tough presumptive limits law, defining the level of alcohol in the blood at which a person is presumed to be drunk. This vital new weapon combatted a lethal menace, since alcohol was involved in 35 percent of all fatal accidents.

(6) New, safer road-design standards went into effect in 1969.

Ron and Nancy at Philadelphia, Pennsylvania

NATURE AND DESIGN

Major consideration for the preservation of scenic and ecological values was a "must" part of the planning of all highways and other state construction. Under Governor Reagan, California:

(1) Established a joint committee of conservation and transportation officials to coordinate efforts to protect the natural environment.

(2) Redesigned freeways to reduce noise levels and protect important parks and natural-beauty areas.

(3) Modified construction projects to avoid disturbing the natural habitat of birds, fish and wildlife.

SENSIBLE BALANCE

To provide the well-balanced transportation system it had to have, California, under Governor Reagan's leadership:

(1) Created a board to review overall transportation programs such as the freeway and expressway system, the State Aviation Master Plan, and regional programs developed by regional agencies.

(2) Advanced the planned starting dates for 1,250 major highway construction projects totaling $380 million, through economics and more-efficient management.

(3) Increased completed freeway and expressway mileage from 2,714 to 3,176 miles in three years.

(4) Cut in half the time for processing driver's license applications.

(5) Retrieved $384 million in US freeway funds ear-
marked for San Francisco, but rejected there. Instead
of reverting to Washington, the state won authority to
use the money on LA's Century Freeway.

The Welfare Bill organized and produced by Ronald Reagan ended up saving taxpayers in California $2 billion. He left
the office of Governor with a great interest in the American
people—a true humanitarian for the state of California.

SIX

Beginning Years as President

THE FIRST TIME he ran for President, against Gerald Ford in 1976, Ronald Reagan lost to five primaries. He told all his supporters, in a speech after losing the first set of primaries, they should remain hopeful for their future. He knew lots of people in America shared his beliefs and hopes.

At the same time, he wrote a time-capsule letter about the events of the USA. It could be reviewed centuries from now and Ronald stated, "I hope whoever reads this will know if we met our challenges." He also spent time working on his beautiful new home and ranch with Nancy. I'm sure his children, Patti and Ronald Prescott, also spent good time with Nancy and Ronald during that time. Enclosed is a picture scene of "Rancho Del Cielo," as they called it. It showed their beautiful home as well as their large lake.

Paid for by Citizens for Reagan, Sen.

"From the first day we saw it, Rancho del Cielo cast a spell over us. No place before or since has ever given Nancy and me the joy and serenity it does. "

-- Ronald Reagan

Rancho Del Cielo

axalt, Chairman, Henry M. Buchanan, Treasurer, 2021 L. St. N.W. Washington, D.C. 20036

A picture of Ronald and Nancy in their boat on the lake.

"President and Mrs. Reagan canoeing across Lake
Lucky at their beloved California ranch, Rancho
del Cielo. The canoe was an anniversary gift
from the President."

PHOTO CREDIT:
Courtesy of the Ronald Reagan Library
8-17-83

This became a project of the Young American's Foundation. It included 688 acres of ground. Here is a great photograph of Ronald and his horse, El Alamein.

Rancho del Cielo means "ranch in the sky." It served as a retreat for President Reagan for over 25 years. It was at this ranch that Ronald, as President, retreated to recharge his batteries and ponder the many great decisions of his career and presidency. He truly loved this beautiful ranch and actually built portions of it himself. No place before or since has given Nancy and Ronald the joy and serenity it provided for them. The ranch was purchased in the spring of 1998 by the Young America's Foundation to be preserved as a living monument to Reagan's legacy and to serve as the centerpiece of the Ronald Reagan Leadership Development Program. It was always important for President Reagan to reach out to young people with his ideas. He addressed the students at one of the foundation's conferences. He stated, "Young America's Foundation has been a refuge for students seeking an alternative to the politically-correct environment enforced on many campuses. I know this conference will send you back to your campuses better informed, motivated, and trained. Your work is vital to the future of the nation." This information was supplied by the Ronald Reagan Library about the ranch's purpose.

In 1980, he campaigned for less government and stronger defense. Supplied information was in his campaign folder entitled, "Let's Make America Great Again." The first statement from Ronald was, "This is a great country, but it's not being run like a great country. That is why I am running for President." He sincerely loved this country and was deeply concerned about the total welfare of the American people. His sincere intention was to recreate people's own American Dream. Economics were terribly high for the American people under Carter's leadership.

When asked, "What about inflation?" Ronald answered, "It's a disaster, because government continues to spend billions of dollars more than it takes in." Ronald Reagan called for a ceiling on Federal spending and a crackdown on waste. At the same time, he favored incentive tax cuts to increase economic productivity. What about the energy crisis? Ronald Reagan believed the United States had to become self-sufficient in energy so no one "could ever blackmail us again." He favored an end to restrictive controls so we could use all the resources available, including more US oil and natural gas. That meant more and prudent use of coal, more nuclear power with strict safeguards and, for the long term, more solar energy and other sources.

What about foreign policies? To preserve peace, Ronald Reagan believed America had to regain leadership of the world. We must build our defense capability, reassure and strengthen our allies and restore our own confidence to defend vital US interests in an increasingly troubled world.

Ronald sincerely tried and worked very hard to fulfill these intentions as President, with the continued welfare of all American people and their future his main goal in mind.

As Governor of California, Ronald had already accomplished, in eight years, proof about what better government can do. By itself, California would be the eighth-largest industrial nation in the world. The state faced bankruptcy when Governor Reagan took office. Asserting his leadership, Governor Reagan turned the state's red ink to black. California had the lowest inflation rate in the US. He also had the same type of aides as governor as he had with strong ideals and motives for the betterment of all people. That is why California came out ahead and with great leadership accomplishment.

Ronald Wilson Reagan was inaugurated as the 40th President of the United States on January 20, 1981. Ronald's Vice-President was George Herbert Walker Bush.

President Ronald Reagan

Chief Justice Warren Earl Burger administered the oath of office for Ronald. For the first time, the ceremony was held at the West Front of the Capital. Ronald gave a 20-minute address, calling for "an era of national renewal" and promising to reduce taxes and control government spending. Minutes later, he fulfilled a campaign promise by placing a freeze on government hiring. As Ronald finished his address, the Iranian government finally released 52 American hostages from Iran, who now were on the final leg of their journey home. This welcome news added to the festive spirit of his inauguration event.

Ronald Reagan's stand on issues:

(1) *Abortion*: Opposed, except when necessary to save a mother's life.

(2) *Nuclear Power:* Favored it; waste disposal problem had been overstated and could be resolved.

(3) *Salt II:* Believed the Senate should declare the treaty fatally flawed, shelve it and negotiations should go back to the table and come up with a treaty which fairly and genuinely reduced the numbers of strategic nuclear weapons.

(4) *US and China Relations:* Favored improved friendship with people of the Chinese Mainland, but not at the expense of Taiwan. Believed President Carter acted hastily and made unnecessary concessions.

(5) *Balanced Budget Amendment:* Had long favored a balanced budget but was concerned that if a balanced budget alone was passed, Congress could raise taxes to match whatever it wanted to spend. Favored first a limitation on tax or spending to curb Congress' appetite.

(6) *Constitutional Conventions:* Amendment method used throughout our history worked and was preferred. However, did not fear a Constitutional Convention as some politicians seemed to. They said it would be "dangerous" to show little faith in American people. Ronald Reagan had great faith, not only in God-given purpose, but great faith in the good people of America and America's future to obtain and keep high ideals for always.

(7) *Inflation:* Its basic cause was government continually spending more than it took in. When government stopped doing that, inflation would get under control.

(8) *Energy Shortage:* Favored deregulation of oil and natural gas to stem domestic sources. Encouraged nuclear power, coal gasification, gasohol, solar, to extents practical.

(9) *Taxes:* Favored income tax cuts to provide incentives to individuals and businesses to strengthen and expand the economy. He was opposed to tax structure that increased taxes at a faster rate than wage increases.

(10) *Foreign Policy:* Clear policy based on national interests with clear understanding of interrelationship of global problems issue.

(11) *Environment:* Favored clean-environment policy, in balance with need for growth, so that all Americans had an opportunity to have a slice of an expanding "pie."

A lot of statistical data is given by the Presidential Encyclopedia from the library, but a lot of the opinions you will read show what real motives Ronald had for his country by me, who knew him.

ATTEMPT ON RONALD REAGAN'S LIFE

President Reagan was shot in the chest as he left the Washington Hilton Hotel on March 30, 1981, after addressing a group of union officials. His assailant, John Warnock Hinckley, Jr., who fired six explosive bullets from a .22 caliber pistol, also wounded the President's secret service agent, Timothy J. McCarthy, and a District of Columbia Policeman, Thomas K. Delahanty. Ronald Reagan was rushed to nearby George Washington University Hospital, where later in the afternoon, he underwent surgery to remove a bullet from his left lung.

Prior to the time of this assassination attempt, when Ronald declared himself a presidential candidate for the 1981 election, I had a dream about Ronald Reagan and saw him being shot before trying to enter a car, and it really terrified me in the dream as I watched it all. I wrote Nancy and Ronald a letter about it and received a telephone call from Nancy thanking me for the letter. She felt the same possibility, but it was necessarily true. But she did declare at that time that, even though he knew of the possibility, Ronald felt he was truly sent from God to care for and free this country.

With more details later on how he completed his mission to save this country from the threatening Communists' Empire, I am going to tell you about what his daughter, Patti, learned from him. This is what she wrote about her father in her book, *Angels Don't Die*. He taught her strong and endless faith in God's purpose. Patti describes Ronald Reagan's faith that she would grow into an adult who never doubted the possibility of miracles and the presence of God, and hears her father answer even when the dark times seem overwhelming. She also stated that he was focused on the most divine aspect of love, that of giving. Patti also stated in her book, "My father told me that Cardinal Cooke assured my father after he was shot in March 1981 that he 'had an angel on his shoulder'." And it makes perfect sense to her now, knowing how close he came to death. The surgeons had a hard time finding the bullet, which was located an inch from his heart when it was found. He also lost a lot of blood. Before he went for the operation, he opened his eyes to Nancy and said, "Honey, I forgot to duck!" Twelve days after being shot and near death, April 11, 1981, he returned to the White House.

1982 Christmas card from White House

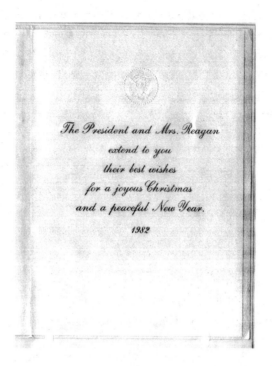

The President and Mrs. Reagan
extend to you
their best wishes
for a joyous Christmas
and a peaceful New Year.

1982

The assailant, John Hinckley, 25 years old, from Evergreen, Colorado, was overpowered and arrested at the scene of the crime. He was sent to Butner Federal Prison, near Raleigh, North Carolina, for psychiatric testing. On June 3, 1982, a jury found Hinckley "not guilty by reason of insanity." He was confined for an indefinite period in St. Elizabeth's Hospital, an institution for the mentally ill.

Patti further states that the day of her father's near-death, "He actually didn't look frail, he looked ethereal. There was a light in his eyes." Her mother told her that after the operation, he woke up, unable to talk because he had a tube down his throat. He saw figures in white standing around him, and wrote on a piece of paper, "I'm alive, aren't I?" Nancy still has the note. They both (Nancy and Patti) thought he just saw nurses standing around him, but later found out that all the nurses working in intensive care wore green scrubs. Then Patti and Nancy believed he had been surrounded by angels, because the bullet found a quarter-inch from his heart had not exploded. He told Patti he knew his physical healing was directly dependent on his ability to forgive John Hinckley, and Patti remembers telling him, "You're the best Christian around." By showing Patti that forgiveness is the key to everything, including physical health and healing, he gave her an example of Christ-like thinking. To Ronald, forgivness is the antidote for anger, fear, and every form of hatred. All that forgiveness naturally leads to miracles. His statement to Patti about forgiving Hinckley was pure and simple, a certainty Ronald thought he would share with the rest of us.

It saddened Patti that much of what passes as Christianity these days is not about Christ-like thinking and is leagues away from forgiveness.

During Ronald Reagan's Administration, some prominent figures from the Religious Right rallied around him and aligned themselves with him. His direct aides in his administration all belonged to the same dogma. Ronald's statement about forgiving the man who shot him demonstrates that he has embraced the essence of Jesus Christ's teachings. Patti never heard his administrative aides say anything remotely resembling that from their religious-right dogma. Ronald said that heroes are frequently people who in everyday life take a moment to help someone else. I do believe that his administrative assistants did not share Ronald's humanitarian interests for betterment of all. That is why, through their and Congress' passing over the high ideals he wanted for the American people, his economic plan did not end up benefiting the American people This caused Ronald Reagan great concern and regret. Also, Patti included in her book, *Angels Don't Die*, that he taught her your true home is with God. He sent us all here, Ronald told her, and someday he'll take us back. Patti knows God will be ready to take her father home at some point, but because of what he taught me and the lesson of faith in which Ronald lived and taught her, Patti knows she will meet him again in heaven. When he frequently referred to John Hinckley as "misguided," he never expressed anger or hatred toward the man who had shot him. He expressed pity. Through true forgiveness, our own sins against God's words, we are then led to forgiveness for all those against us. That kind of forgiveness transforms and heals. Lives can then be constructed from love, rather than from fear or vengeance.

During Ronald Reagan's recovery, he believed he was spared for a reason—the same reason he entered the presidency. After the attempt on his life, Ronald said, "The rest of my days belong to God." He knew he had more work to do for Him. Patti Davis' life continues to change as a result of the lessons her father taught her. She feels her spirit reshape itself around her father's words.

Mother Theresa stated to him that God had a planned reason for him to suffer. Ronald became even more evangelical and set examples that forgiveness for all others against us can lead to our own healing and God's purpose for us.

Nancy asked Mike Dever, "Please see that this never happens again." And it did not. Four weeks after Ronald recovered, he received a hero's welcome from Congress.

REAGANOMICS AND THE ECONOMY

On August 13, 1981, Ronald Reagan signed a bill he thought was bringing the conservative agenda into law. Unfortunately, the bill that was passed did not include a balanced budget. He tried for further tax cuts, but the economy did not do well for the people, to his deep regret. When Reagan took office in 1981, during a prolonged period of so-called "stagflation," inflation reached 11.2 percent and interest rates had soared to 20 percent. Those circumstances contributed to Reagan's victory over Jimmy Carter. In early 1981, statistics of unemployment and inflation rates stood at 20.7 percent.

1983 Christmas card from White House

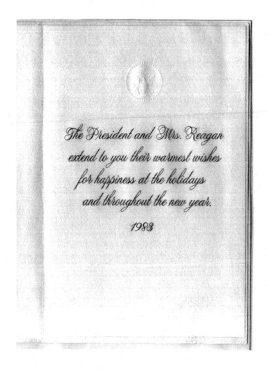

The President and Mrs. Reagan
extend to you their warmest wishes
for happiness at the holidays
and throughout the new year.

1988

The President's plan to stimulate the economy while cutting inflation—a version of supply-side economics, popularly dubbed "Reaganomics"—combined a three-stage tax cut with a tightened money supply and deep cuts in federal spending for social programs, including funding for health, food, housing and education. The nation underwent a severe recession. By late 1982, unemployment hit a 42-year high of 10.6 percent, with almost 12 million people out of work. In 1983, the poverty rate reached its highest point in 18 years. Through 1982, effects were felt against the American homeless; they had increased. So did unemployment increase.

Ronald stated, "I prayed a lot for the whole country and asked for help and guidance to do the right thing. I need a miracle." (Less government, lower taxes.)

Ronald sent personal checks to people who wrote to him while on welfare, telling them not to save them but cash them for their personal benefits.

On November 2, voters voted against Republican Congress, which upset Ronald. The President then supported the tight-money policies of Paul Volcker, the head of the Federal Reserve Board, who had been appointed by Jimmy Carter. The harsh medicine prescribed by Volcker helped to cure the ailing economy—the answer to Ronald's prayers. By late 1984, inflation was down to 4.3 percent and unemployment stood at 7.4 percent—the same rate it was when Reagan took office. Personal and industrial income had increased substantially, and the stock market reached record heights. Ronald Reagan's landslide victory over Walter Mondale, in 1984, was due in part to this economic boom.

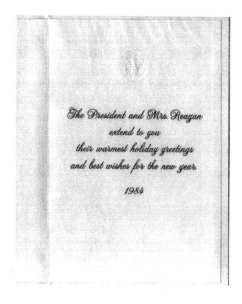

1984 Christmas card from White House

At the end of the President's tenure, the inflation rate was a manageable 4.4 percent and unemployment had fallen to 5.3 percent, the lowest rate since 1974. Moreover, during an unprecedented peacetime expansion of the economy, which began in November 1982, more than 15 million new jobs had been created and the number of workers earning more than the minimum wage had been reduced to 22 percent.

Ronald Reagan's response on all the economy issues was to tell all that the deficit was to blame the Congress for all their wanton social spending and to reiterate his support for a balanced budget amendment to the Constitution. Of all the six budgets (1981–1986) that produced a huge deficit, 94 percent was proposed by Congress and Ronald Reagan's aides at that time—not at all the goals and opportunities for the people of America that Ronald truly wanted. I was still sending and receiving Christmas cards from Ronald and Nancy.

SEVEN

Result of Ronald Reagan's Humanitarian Efforts

RONALD REAGAN VOWED to fight against communism to free the entire world. To fight communism's position in the world and to be on equal footing, he declared a Nuclear Weapons production. He used that upgrade to negotiate with Mikhail Gorbachev. He did not intentionally trade weapons for hostages. He never lost faith in America's creativity. He still had the goal and incentive to end the Cold War. He felt (and I felt) he was sent by God to America to conquer the evil empire for the world, communism.

It cost America a great amount of money. Many people called the President a warmonger because of his support of all the countries dominated by Communists. But he truly wanted to help support and bring Communists to the point where they had to end the Cold War. Our strong military and nuclear buildup from him reached the same average as Mikhail Gorbachev's. Our strength after the nuclear and military buildup (including a raise of salary for all our military forces) was on the same negotiation level to lead to its success of ending the Cold War. He was supported by important leaders, such as Margaret Thatcher. You can believe the high esteem she felt about him by seeing the picture of Ronald Reagan and Margaret Thatcher.

15/450

"Today we are particularly conscious of the courage of Ronald Reagan. It was easy for his contemporaries to ignore it: He always seemed so calm and relaxed, with natural charm, unstudied self-assurance, and unquench-able good humour. He was always ready with just the right quip – often self-deprecatory, though with a seri-ous purpose – so as to lighten the darkest moments and give all around him heart."

Lady Margaret Thatcher
December 10, 1997

"We have every right to dream heroic dreams. Those who say that we're in a time when there are no heroes, they just don't know where to look. They're the individ-uals and families whose taxes support the government and whose voluntary gifts support church, charity, cul-ture, art and education. Their patriotism is deep. Their values sustain our national life."

President Ronald Reagan
Inaugural Address
January 20, 1981

He did push the Soviet Union to the point of collapse. Even the Pope, John Paul II, thought Ronald Reagan indeed had a special mission for the people of the United States of America. His advisors and aides were not always on his side, nor did they always share the high ideals he had. Weapons buildup was madness to a lot of people. Even his own daughter, Patti, criticized him for the arms and nuclear buildup and support to other countries fighting Communist domination.

You must realize that Ronald had Armageddon in mind with achieving an agreement with Mikhail Gorbachev. Ronald had to destroy the effects of nuclear defense by communism by his total buildup. Then, when Ronald and Gorbachev signed the agreement of "No Nuclear War," Ronald saved the world from a potential Armageddon.

One of Ronald's favorite songs, which he endorsed, was "God Bless the USA," and "I'm Proud To Be An American." He loved and dedicated himself to this country, the USA.

On March 8, 1983, Ronald called the Soviet Union an "evil empire" and Soviet Communism, "the focus of evil in the modern world." Two weeks later, he proposed the Strategic Defense Initiative, a new laser beam-operated defensive shield—popularly known as "Star Wars"—that could destroy enemy missiles and warheads in space. To counter the Soviet deployment in Warsaw block countries of SS-20 medium-range missiles aimed at Western Europe, the United States deployed cruise missiles and medium-range nuclear missiles in five NATO countries during the fall of 1983, despite mass protest in those countries and in the United States. On November 23, 1983, a week after the first cruise missiles were installed in Great Britain, the Soviets withdrew from the arms control negotiations in which they and the United States had been participating since 1981.

As the 1984 presidential election approached and Reagan's re-election seemed certain, he and the Soviets adopted a more conciliatory attitude. Early in 1985, Secretary of State George C. Schultz met with Soviet Foreign Secretary Andrei Grumyko for talks that produced an agreement to begin arms control negotiations in March 1985. And, when 54-year-old Mikhail S. Gorbachev was elected to the position of General Secretary of the Communist Party, President Reagan sought a meeting with him. The President had known better than to try to negotiate with Breznhev, Andropov and Chernoko.

Economic deterioration of the Soviet Union strengthened Gorbachev's hand with the Central Committee of the Communist Party when he espoused the policies called *glasnost*—the opening of the Soviet Society and a call for the eventual transfer of some power from the Communist Party to popularly elected bodies—and *perestroika*, an economic restructuring that lessened state control and introduced some Free-Market practices.

Ronald became optimistic about these developments. The Reagan Administration agreed to four superpower summit meetings during Ronald's second term. They were held in Geneva, Rejhyavick, Washington, DC, and Moscow.

The most significant result of this thaw in US-Soviet relations took place in Washington, DC, in December 1987, when Reagan and Gorbachev signed the most sweeping arms control agreement in modern history. The Intermediate-Range Nuclear Force (INF) treaty, eliminating medium-range missiles, was the first agreement between the "superpowers" to reduce their nuclear stockpiles. It led to the destruction of approximately 2,600 warheads over an 18-month period and, for the first time, permitted the on-site inspection of nuclear missile facilities in the Soviet Union and in the United States.

The Reagan Doctrine was the name given to the President's policy of offering support—convert (CIA to anti-

Soviet Afghan rebels, for example) as well as overt—to-anti-communist insurgencies in the Third World. Since the late 1940s, American policy had aimed to contain Soviet expansionism. But Ronald Reagan sought to roll back communism in countries where unpopular regimes were propped up by the Soviets, or by Soviet client-states like Cuba. The forces of the 1980s that coalesced to thwart the spread of totalitarianism had been gathering strength over many years, but the Reagan Doctrine, itself, produced tangible results. The Soviet Union withdrew from Afghanistan, the Vietnamese began their retreat from Cambodia, and the Cubans agreed to pull out of Angola.

The ideological component of the Reagan Doctrine stated that social programs are tied to the development of markets and face markets require political liberty. That argument was forcefully advanced by both the President and his frequent ally in Europe, Prime Minister Margaret Thatcher of Great Britain. I did tell you that Margaret Thatcher was a tremendous supporter of Ronald Reagan's policies to defeat communism.

President Reagan's policy in Central America was to contain the spread of communism by both open and covert activities. In El Salvador, the administration sent massive amounts of military and economic aid to the Christian Democratic government of Jose Napoleon Duarte. In Nicaragua, the Reagan Administration provided funds, arms and training to the Contra—rebels dedicated to overthrowing the Marxist Sandinista government.

President Reagan and Congress often clashed over funding for the Contras. Despite calling Contra leaders the "moral equivalent of our founding fathers," the President was unable to convince the public that Nicaragua posed a serious threat to political stability in Central America.

In October 1986, the President prevailed upon Congress to lift its ban and sent the Contras $100 million in military aid. Less than a month later, it was revealed that the administration had been secretly selling arms since 1985 to Iran in exchange for Iranian assistance in freeing American hostages from captivity in Lebanon. In late November, an embarrassing problem blew up into a political crisis for the administration. It came to light that Iran had been overcharged for the weapons and that the profits had been diverted to the Contras by operatives working on the staff of the National Security Council. After it became known, Rear Admiral Poindexter, Chief of NSC, resigned, and Lieutenant Colonel Oliver North was dismissed.

A preliminary investigation by Attorney General Edward Messe disclosed that between $10 million and $30 million had been diverted from arms sales profits, though President Reagan knew nothing about the scheme. Poindexter testified under oath that he, and not the President, had authorized the diversion of Iranian arms sales profits. Because the operation was politically explosive, he said he deliberately did not tell the President about the diversions. I'm sure Ronald would not have approved of such tactics.

Ronald should have showed everyone by that time that he really cared about human rights. And you cannot compromise with evil such as the Soviet theology. Homeless people had multiplied, and unemployment rose to a new, overwhelming high. It certainly did upset Ronald Reagan to the point where he sent his own personal checks to people on unemployment. He still possessed high ideals for his fellow man.

Important Dates: on December 7–10, 1987, Gorbachev and Reagan met in Washington, DC, signing the INF treaty—the first arms treaty to cut the superpowers' nuclear arsenals. Ronald Reagan's build-up-to-tear-down worked. It was the collapse of Soviet Communism. Ronald never made idle threats to them, but he urged the Soviets to believe and control their own human rights and pushed them to seek more religious freedom in the Soviet Union. He did start to trust Gorbachev. In 1988, the complete Cold War was ended; all Soviet forces left Afghanistan. In 1989, the Berlin Wall came down. The Iron Curtain was also removed and still remains down.

Ronald's primary goal was to force America away from big government. He truly was a very strong, well-intentioned man. He joined every organization that was out to save the world. He knew how the Communist menace tried to control everyone's lives, because of having being an informant for the USA while being president of the SAG.

Ronald did believe everything happened for a reason. To fight communism and big government was his goal.

Billy Graham was a close acquaintance of Ronald's, and Ronald respected all the things he told him. Billy Graham stated that Ronald was a proven winner all his life. Ronald's Christian beliefs were based on his mother, Moms Nelle's. They both belonged to the Christian church in Dixon, Illinois, that was Disciples of Christ. All beliefs were based on the Bible and the belief that when having faith, the Hand of God, through Jesus Christ, directs your life.

In knowing all these facts now, when the rising economy skyrocketed under his administration, it thoroughly disturbed and led him to end up getting new administrative associates to help him reach his high ideals for the American people. He stated, "I prayed a lot for this country, and for help and guidance to do the right thing. I needed a miracle of less government, lower taxes. And, that's what I sincerely strive to do."

Through the Contra Revolution that Ronald did know about, diversion of funds, he knew he was not in control of his aides in his administration. Poindexter fired both North and Don Regan. This happened in 1987 and was very troubling for Ronald Reagan to think he lost public appeal. Howard Baker was hired to replace Don Regan because Regan was not in agreement and cooperation with Ronald Reagan. Even Vice-President Bush stated and knew that to be true.

Ronald Reagan became in full control of his aides and government. Howard Baker was fully capable in his job. Ronald's former aides did not hold his high ideals and motives. Ronald later admitted that there were weapons for hostages, not what he intended but what developed after the assassination attempt against him.

In October 1987, Gorbachev signed the complete agreement to reduce all the weapons and the threat of nuclear war. Ronald Reagan's build-up-to-build-down worked to collapse Soviet Communism. Then, as stated before, within the same agreement, Gorbachev tore down the Berlin Wall and the Iron Curtain.

Ronald Reagan never made idle threats. He pushed for more human rights and more religious freedom to the Soviet people, and encouraged the Soviets to undermine the communist rule.

Ronald started to trust Gorbachev, and in 1988, the Cold War was ended. In 1989, Soviet forces left Afghanistan. Also in 1989, the Berlin Wall came down permanently. In 1991, Gorbachev dissolved the Soviet Union.

Now, no one can deny or not give credit to Ronald Reagan—a most competent President.

He left the White House in 1989, when he was 78 years old. His daughter, Patti, wrote her book, *Angels Don't Die* after he left office.

In November 5, 1994, he wrote and told all his people about his having Alzheimer's disease. He stated in his letter that he was leaving with great love for this country and great hope for its future. He closed with "May God always bless you. Sincerely, Ronald Reagan."

Ronald also experienced two severe health problems during his last four years in office. On July 13, 1985, he had a malignant colon polyp removed. He also experienced severe prostate illness. He survived both of them and went on trying to save this country and the rest of the world from communism. And he did.

He also enacted, on January 29, 1988, administration prohibiting federally-funded family-planning centers from providing any assistance to women seeking abortions. Again, Ronald was putting his country into a Christian ideal, knowing that abortion was not ever the holy will of God.

When Ronald left office on January 20, 1989, he left with opinion polls showing him to be the most popular president since Franklin D. Roosevelt.

He is now experiencing severe illness, suffering from Alzheimer's. It is terribly hard for this gifted communicator not to be able to do that any more. His public acknowledgment helped lift the stigma many people associated with Alzheimer's. As Nancy stated, they did not know it was a disease. He helped many people to be free to talk about it now. He did a great thing. Ronald's wife, Nancy, learned to deal with her husband's condition. She said, "You just do it. You just get up and take each day as it comes and put one foot in front of the other. You just love." I personally think that her help and support to Ron, ever since he began suffering the effects of this disease, has been a good example of her loyalty and dedication to Ronald. Now it is truly hard for her, because she cannot even have a conversation that makes any sense with him now.

To begin with, Nancy Davis Reagan was a stylish and sociable First Lady, with a flair for lavish entertainment. She gave up her movie career to be a dedicated wife to Ronald. She gained valuable experience in public life as the wife of the Governor of California. She took up charity work as her project and proved to be a skillful and indefatigable companion. Nancy Reagan started her career by studying drama at Smith College, worked in Broadway Theater, and then went to Hollywood. She appeared in 11 films before she retired from movies. The movie she and Ronald shared was *Hellcats of the Navy*, in 1957. It was the last motion picture for both of them.

As First Lady, Mrs. Reagan was prominently involved in the campaign against illegal drugs. She visited drug rehabilitation centers, sponsored drug-education programs in public schools, and helped to popularize the slogan "just say no." She emphasized the elimination of demand for drugs, more than cutting off the sources of their supply. Although Ronald was an immensely genial man, while President, Ronald is said to have had no time for anyone except his wife as his best friend.

Mrs. Reagan had run-ins with his advisers because she knew they had deflated his general upbeat mode, or tried to knock him off his confident stride and high ideals. Nancy certainly knew the loyal, Christian hard worker for the American people. Sharing the stage with him for eight years, she was—in many ways—the President's unwavering loyal co-star.

By now, I hope you have learned the true humanitarian Ronald was all his life.

Bibliography

Hubler, Richard G., and Ronald Reagan. *Where's the Rest of Me: The Ronald Reagan Story*. Hollywood: Duell, Sloan and Pearce, Publisher Affiliate of Meredith Press. 1965.

Kent, Zachary. *Ronald Reagan: Fortieth President of the United States (Encyclopedia of Presidents)*.Conneticutt: Children's Press. 1989.

Levy, Peter. *Encyclopedia of Reagan-Bush Years*. Westport, CT: Greenwood Press. 1996.

The Presidents. "Ronald Reagan's Full Encyclopedia." New York: Simon and Schuster Macmillan. 1997.